"Wilson labors to make us appreciate the greatness and grandeur of the gospel and its Christ. Again and again he succeeds."

J. I. Packer, Board of Governors' Professor of Theology, Regent College; author, *Knowing God*

"Too many of us treat the gospel as somebody else's news. We know it's what saved us, but we encounter it only as we overhear ourselves rehearsing it to unbelievers. Or, we treat the gospel as some law of supernatural quantum physics—holding everything together but too complicated to think about very much. That's a dry, flat, and depressing way to live. This brilliant, winsome book calls us back to the exhilarating bigness of the gospel, in a way that can spark up every day with crucified power. Read this book. It's like a gospel fountain flowing, deep and wide."

Russell D. Moore, Dean, School of Theology; Senior Vice President for Academic Administration; Professor of Theology and Ethics, The Southern Baptist Theological Seminary

"This is good leaf, grown with gospel sap, grounded in Bible soil. Drop this fresh bag from Jared in your soul's mug, and give it a good steep. As good as the flavor was in *Gospel Wakefulness*, it's even better in *Gospel Deeps*."

David Mathis, executive editor, desiringGod.org; elder, Bethlehem Baptist Church, Twin Cities, Minnesota

"If your faith in Christ is shallow, this is not the book for you. But if you are suffering, if you are sinning, if you are broken, and you need a big Savior, Jared Wilson's *Gospel Deeps* might take you deeper with Christ than you've ever gone before, deeper than you've ever dreamed of going. Enjoy the journey."

Ray Ortlund, Immanuel Church, Nashville, Tennessee

"Jared Wilson's *Gospel Deeps* is not just another book on the Christian life, it is a book on what gives the Christian life—the gospel. And it isn't a mere summary of the gospel, but a plunge deep into the good news to help the reader understand the gospel's centrality and power in our lives. *Gospel Deeps* helps us behold and experience the glory and goodness of Jesus Christ in ways we often forget, or may be completely unfamiliar with."

Joe Thorn, author, *Note to Self: The Discipline of Preaching to Yourself*; Lead Pastor, Redeemer Fellowship, St. Charles, Illinois

"Those without spiritual eyes will not enjoy Jared's book. How could they? All he does is stare deeply into the person of Jesus Christ and his gospel work. But for those with eyes to see, what treasures await here. Jared gazes upon the gospel from angle after angle, showing how every area of theology points back to the gospel, and reminding us that the knowledge of God is like a spiderweb—where touching any one spot makes the whole thing vibrate. Jared, like the best theologians, worships as he writes and invites readers to join him. And that means this pastor-theologian's pen is a lyrical one. Read slowly, enjoy, savor, and worship."

Jonathan Leeman, Editorial Director, 9Marks; author, *Church and the Surprising Offense of God's Love*

"Wilson's *Gospel Deeps* offers a majestic portrait of the gospel that is far more than a solution to guilt or a one-time gate to forgiveness. It's a path we are to walk each day of our lives, an answer to the moral corruption of our culture and entire cosmos, the power to change us into authentic worshipers of God and lovers of people, and a supernatural power given to the church to bring healing to a broken world. Multifaceted in its reflection of the many spiritual blessings promised to those united with Christ, *Gospel Deeps* compels us to revel anew in the excellencies of Jesus."

Steve Childers, President and CEO, Global Church Advancement; Associate Professor of Practical Theology, Reformed Seminary Orlando

"The gospel of Jesus Christ offers to us spiritual riches that exceed our wildest imaginations. *Gospel Deeps* is a delightful ledger of sorts to these riches. As one of the top writers in the church today, Jared Wilson labors hard to surface great gospel truth with clarity and brilliance, and in language that carries with it a steady overtone of delight. He says it well: 'If Christ is true then boredom is a sin.' Yes! And because Christ is true, and because Jared knows it, I dare you to find a boring page in this book."

Tony Reinke, author, *Lit! A Christian Guide to Reading Books*

"First of all, a given: Jared Wilson is one of the finest and brightest young pastors and gospel thinkers in America. Second, a nongiven: Jared is still growing. What excites me most about *Gospel Deeps* is that it represents the trajectory of a heart that is continuing to come alive to the implications of the gospel. In this book, Jared is not just our gifted teacher, but also our worship leader. He bids us join him in putting our roots deeper and deeper into the garden of God's grace. Thank you, my brother, for theology as doxology."

Scotty Smith, Founding Pastor, Christ Community Church, Franklin, TN

"If you have assumed that doctrine must be dull, cool, or cerebral, *Gospel Deeps* will disabuse you of that notion. If you think that passionate adoration and deep dogmas—sovereign election, double imputation, inaugurated eschatology—don't belong together, *Gospel Deeps* will surprise you by its blend of worshipful warmth with theological profundity. If you are beginning to realize that growing up in Christ does not mean getting *beyond* the gospel but going *more deeply into* it, exploring the implications of Jesus's sacrificial death and resurrection on our behalf, *Gospel Deeps* will energize your pursuit of holiness by fortifying your assurance of the Father's unwavering love and glad acceptance. If you thirst to know the triune God who saves you, *Gospel Deeps* will lead you into the Word by which he reveals himself and invites us into communion with himself. Plunge into these deeps!"

Dennis E. Johnson, Professor of Practical Theology, Westminster Seminary, California; author, *Him We Proclaim*; coauthor, *Counsel from the Cross*

OTHER CROSSWAY BOOKS BY JARED C. WILSON

The Explicit Gospel (with Matt Chandler)

Gospel Wakefulness

GOSPEL DEEPS

Reveling in the Excellencies of Jesus

JARED C. WILSON

FOREWORD BY MATT CHANDLER

:: CROSSWAY

WHEATON, ILLINOIS

Library of Congress Cataloging-in-Publication Data

Wilson, Jared C., 1975–
   Gospel deeps : reveling in the excellencies of Jesus /
     Jared C. Wilson.
     p. cm.
   Includes bilographical references and index.
   ISBN 978-1-4335-2640-4
    1. Salvation—Christianity. 2. Jesus Christ—Person and
offices. I. Title.
BT751.3.W545   2012
234—dc23   2012013350

For my wife, Becky, again.
Because every day you love me, again.
You are the daily picture of grace to me.

Contents

Foreword

God is big, weighty, thick, immense. This is no cliché, although we could make it one. God is so big that to dwell on his immensity long enough could lead one into terror. In the display of his glory God is beyond overwhelming. We sense God's bigness in his interaction with his creation. For instance, as many of us as there are—eight billion at last count—he nevertheless knows us all, even, according to Matthew 10:30, down to the number of hairs we have (or don't have) on our heads. He knows our personal histories and all of our thoughts past, present, and future and all of our feelings and motivations and needs and desires, and how all the moments in our lives have led to the person we are this very second as we hold this book. The elements obey him, and even a sparrow doesn't fall out of the sky unless he allows it. I have no idea how many sparrows there are but I'm guessing they are right up there with us humans, if they don't outnumber us. That's a lot of activity! And God is all over all of it.

As if that weren't big and thick and immense enough, against the broader scope of the universe, our earth is tiny, and we are of course even smaller. Though we believe it to be so massive and unending, this green and blue ball of ours is actually a tiny blue speck in God's grand display of his eternal might. We are a small planet surrounded by an immeasurable amount of space that includes millions of larger planets and celestial bodies that dwarf what we define as "big." As far as earth goes—and this is being generous—we are a small ant pile in the middle of the Sahara. The prophet Job tells us that this entire expansive universe is but the outskirts or fringes of God's power. I have often marveled at the fact that David didn't know the half of it when he wrote in Psalm 8:

> When I look at your heavens, the work of your fingers,
>> the moon and the stars, which you have set in place,
> what is man that you are mindful of him,
>> and the son of man that you care for him? (vv. 3–4)

David didn't have the images from the Hubble telescope or a strong understanding of just how big the universe really is, but he marveled that the eternal God who had created such an immense universe spared thoughts for mankind. I wonder what David would have written had he known the even bigger picture— had he known the universe's immensity with the help of satellite imagery and astronomic charts.

When I say that dwelling for long on God's immensity could lead one into terror, I have in mind our smallness in light of his holiness. Isaiah knew the feeling well, as God's glory filled the temple (Isaiah 6) and Isaiah felt "undone," as if he might break or explode or melt into a puddle at the very subsuming presence of the perfect radiance of God. C. S. Lewis writes:

> The real test of being in the presence of God is that you either forget about yourself altogether or see yourself as a small, dirty object.

The fact that God sustains and maintains the universe and beyond without the slightest strain on his abilities should make us draw back, vulnerably in tune with our impossible smallness and fragility. How do you communicate with this God? If you don't like how he's wired things or you're not amenable to what he commands, what could you possibly do about it? We are plankton shaking a microscopic fist at a killer whale.

Yet he hears us. He takes note. He is, the Bible says, "mindful" of us. And *that* should awe us (Ps. 8:4; Heb. 2:6).

Because as big and mighty as God is in light of the universe, the declaration of glory in the heavens is still not where he has most beautifully flexed his muscle. God reveals his power most fully not in the expanse of the universe but rather in his rescuing of those ants in that tiny mound in the middle of the Sahara, by being for them all they couldn't be and taking from them what they could never be rid of. The depth, width, ferocity, and immensity of God is seen most spectacularly in the gospel of Jesus Christ.

I have found in the last decade of pastoral ministry that people tend to understand the "width" of the gospel in that they can describe Jesus and the cross, but they have trouble with the "depth" of the gospel, struggling to see how it informs and shapes every aspect of our lives. In *Gospel Deeps*, my friend Jared does a masterful job of taking us into the depths of God's biggest, weightiest, thickest, most immense plan for the universe and for us, the princes of it. I'm glad you have this book in your hands, and I am praying that the Spirit will show you through it the many glories of God in the rich depths of the message of Christ.

Matt Chandler

Acknowledgments

This book could not have been written without the prayers, wisdom, and loving dedication of friends new and old: David and Sarah McLemore, Ray Ortlund, Chris Booth, Rob Townshend, Jeremy Veldman, Dale Carr, Mike Krohn, Bill Streger, and Matt Chandler; and Josh Cousineau, Mark Gedicks, and the other righteous brothers of the Gospel Alliance New England.

Trevin Wax, Burk Parsons, Dane Ortlund, Joel Burdeaux, and Robert Peterson all offered invaluable insights into the crafting of this or that portion of the manuscript. What is good is better for their refinement; what is bad is the result of my stubbornness.

I am especially grateful to the church communities that have graciously allowed me to audition some of this material in various forms in front of their people over the last couple of years. Thank you Conroe Church of Christ in Conroe, Texas; New Life Church in Gahanna, Ohio; St. John the Divine Episcopal Church in Houston, Texas; Grace Church in Brockton, Massachusetts; and East Auburn Baptist Church in Auburn, Maine, where the Gospel Alliance holds the LEAD Conference, a venue that has endured my thinking aloud most readily.

Most especially I am grateful to and for Middletown Springs Community Church, my own church family. Thank you, dear brothers and sisters, for "going where the gospel goes," with me, and for receiving God's Word with gladness and submission time and time again. It is so fun to revel in the God-ness of God with you!

Introduction

"For from his fullness we have all received,
grace upon grace."—John 1:16

My driving conviction in this book is that the gospel of Jesus Christ is big. Like, *really big*. Ginormous, if you will. And deep. Deep and rich. And beautiful. Multifaceted. Expansive. Powerful. Overwhelming. Mysterious. But vivid, too, and clear. Illuminating. Transforming. And did I mention big?

I grew up in a Southern Baptist church in the Bible Belt. We were conservative, biblical, evangelistic, and invitational. Not a Sunday school class, worship service, Wednesday evening prayer meeting, youth group function, retreat, camp, or potluck went by that we weren't given an opportunity to receive the gospel. No matter what the topic of the gathering might be, we could always count on being invited to raise a hand or walk an aisle at the end. And that is not in itself necessarily a bad thing. Many of us point to experiences just like that as the moment of our conversion to Christ. And the preaching of the gospel should always come with an invitation (of sorts) to repent and believe in it.

As I look back now, however, I hear a scratching of a needle on a record when I think of those invitations. I hear a car screeching to a halt and changing gears. Why? Why do those moments now seem jarring to me? I think it is because the invitation time did not often follow the preaching of the gospel; it followed the preaching of something else. Something biblical, of course. Something helpful. Something practical. Something spiritual. But not the gospel. In fact, what these invitation times began to train people like me to think is that the gospel is *only* for these invitation times. The sort of preaching I grew up with—sincere, experienced, Bible-based, sometimes even expository—inadvertently taught me that the gospel is for the evangelizing of unbelievers only, not for the already convinced.

On top of that, as responses to invitations waned, the alternative was not to take evangelism outside the church or even develop ways of educating and edifying believers in the gospel, but to find new ways to insinuate that believers weren't really believers, that perhaps their sins and struggles required their "getting saved" again. The same preachers who were adamant about the doctrine of eternal security put a lot of rhetorical weight behind cultivating insecurity. In this way, the gospel ceased being the power of God and began becoming the magic formula for a clean slate.

Raised in the church, I heard lots of preaching and teaching. I did not lack one bit for information on the Scriptures. But I was never introduced to the concept of the gospel's bigness. We did not have the gospel *wrong*, really. We just had it shallow. I didn't understand that the gospel was for all of life. If I had read Paul's reminder in 1 Corinthians 15:3 that the gospel of Jesus's death and resurrection is "of first importance," I would have assumed he meant it was a first step.

Obviously the gospel is the ABCs of salvation. But it is also the A to Z.

We had the knowledge of the gospel but we denied the power thereof.

In 1 Corinthians 2:2, Paul tells the church in Corinth, "For I decided to know nothing among you except Jesus Christ and him crucified." Seems a simple enough thing to only know. A few verses later, however, he writes:

> But we impart a secret and hidden wisdom of God, which God decreed before the ages for our glory. None of the rulers of this age understood this, for if they had, they would not have crucified the Lord of glory. But, as it is written,
>
> > "What no eye has seen, nor ear heard,
> >   nor the heart of man imagined,
> > what God has prepared for those who love him"—
>
> these things God has revealed to us through the Spirit. For the Spirit searches everything, even the depths of God. (1 Cor. 2:7–10)

Oo, boy, now we're talking *big*. That same simple knowledge—"Jesus Christ and him crucified"—is also the secret and hidden wisdom from God. The knowledge of Jesus and his atoning work is, Paul tells us, "the depths." The central problem with the evangelical church's mostly truncated gospel (or its simply transactional gospel formula) is that it misses out on these depths. Indeed, it does not evidence knowing that these depths are even there!

I own a MacBook Pro. I like my MacBook Pro a lot. It does the things I want a computer to do. I use it for sending and receiving e-mail, surfing the web, writing blog posts and articles and books, and occasionally listening to music or watching movies. People who know the subject of computers, however, will tell you that if all you want to do is e-mail, surf the Internet, and do some word processing, you probably don't want a MacBook Pro. (Mine came to me used and was a going-away gift from my former church, so I did not overspend.) One day a friend asked if he could use my computer for a minute. I said sure. And then I watched him do things on my computer I didn't know it could do. He opened up programs I didn't even know I had. There are things on this computer that, when accessed, look really, really cool. And as I type these words right now, I have no idea how to see that coolness again. I know I have widgets on this thing, but I have no idea what widgets are, really. People make really nice looking movies on MacBook Pros. I have GarageBand, which everyone says is awesome, but for which I have no use and about which I have no clue. All of this potential sits on my desk or in my lap whenever I open up this machine, but I don't have the slightest notion where it is or how to use it. Similarly, we evangelicals love the gospel for the few of its uses we're aware of, and we end up missing its depths.

We like that our gospel gets our sins forgiven and gives us a ticket to heaven, but we're not sure of its functionality in our lives every day. Many of us don't think of the gospel as applying to marriage or parenting or friendships or even to more explicitly theological subjects the way other categories of information and skill-sets do. We're content to keep the gospel at an elementary level, assuming that we graduate from it, and the sad result of this neglect is that we thereby deny the "grace upon grace" in the fullness of Jesus. There is one gospel, as there is one Jesus, but there are many facets to this gospel, as there are infinite excellencies in Jesus.

The further into the gospel we go, then, the bigger it gets. There is no way for us to wear it out.

In the closing pages of C. S. Lewis's *The Last Battle*, our heroes find themselves in the throes of glorious reunion in a great garden. Like many locales in Aslan's Narnia, the scene without can belie the scene within, as Lucy Pevensie discovers. Looking over the garden wall to a panoramic view, she speaks to her old friend, Tumnus the Faun:

> "I see," she said at last, thoughtfully. "I see now. This garden is like the Stable. It is far bigger inside than it was outside."
>
> "Of course, Daughter of Eve," said the Faun. "The further up and the further in you go, the bigger everything gets. The inside is larger than the outside."
>
> Lucy looked hard at the garden and saw that it was not really a garden at all but a whole world, with its own rivers and woods and sea and mountains. But they were not strange: she knew them all.
>
> "I see," she said. "This is still Narnia, and, more real and more beautiful than the Narnia down below, just as *it* was more real and more beautiful than the Narnia outside the Stable door! I see . . . world within world, Narnia within Narnia. . . . "
>
> "Yes," said Mr. Tumnus, "like an onion: except that as you continue to go in and in, each circle is larger than the last."[1]

The gospel of Jesus Christ's atoning work on the cross and out of the tomb is like this. The further into Christ's work we press, the more of our vision and the more of our heart it fills. Of course, an onion pales as the gospel's symbol, just as my MacBook does. In the Scriptures, we find God's prophets too overwhelmed by the glory of God in the gospel's bigness to offer such miniscule metaphors. When Job gets a glimpse of the enormity of God's sovereign plan for him and for all creation, he says, "I have uttered what I did not

---

[1] C. S. Lewis, *The Last Battle* (New York: Macmillan, 1970), 180.

understand, things too wonderful for me, which I did not know" (Job 42:3). Even King David, no stranger to waxing poetic about all manner of things above and below, ponders God's expansive greatness and uses the phrase "too wonderful" (Ps. 139:6). Paul tells us in Ephesians 3:8 that the riches of Christ are "unsearchable." The biblical writers don't even try to come up with object illustrations: they just stagger. Leon Morris writes, "The New Testament writers are like men who ransack their vocabulary to find words which will bring out some small fraction of the mighty thing that God has done for us."[2]

Still, all of that is to say that it is fine and fitting to search out symbols and metaphors—diamonds, oceans, even Narnian stables and common onions—to reflect the grandness of the gospel, but we ought to own up right away to the reality that none of these objects *fits*. The gospel is contained in an announcement of something Jesus did inside of history. It can even be tweeted in less than 140 characters! But it is nonetheless bigger than the universe.

We must get this. And we have to understand that not getting it is not just an informational "miss." Venturing into the depths of the gospel—seeing Christ's accomplishment (the gospel's content) and what is accomplished by his accomplishment (the gospel's implications)—is vital to better knowing and loving God. When we miss the depths of the gospel, we hinder our worship. In reflecting on how the good news of Jesus creates the people of God, Paul cries out, "Oh, the depth of the riches and wisdom and knowledge of God! How unsearchable are his judgments and how inscrutable his ways!" (Rom. 11:33).

What is Paul doing? He's not just pontificating. He's not just ruminating. He's worshiping! He's exulting. "Oh!" he cries, in response to the bigness of the gospel. Through the good news, Paul receives a clearer and clearer—and larger and larger—vision of God's glory and God's plan.

My previous book, *Gospel Wakefulness*, is mostly about the experience of personal revival and how that applies to multiple areas of the Christian life. Now, in *Gospel Deeps*, I want to explore the

---

[2] Leon Morris, *The Cross in the New Testament* (Grand Rapids, MI: Eerdmans, 1965), 419.

gospel itself, holding it up like a diamond and examining some of its facets. Our look into the depths of the gospel cannot be merely to know more information, as if deciphering some secret code, but instead to seek more and more to be awed by what God has done for us in Christ, what God is doing for us in Christ, and what God *will* do for us in Christ. Plumbing the depths of the gospel is an exultational pursuit, or it is a pointless one.

Come, let us reason together. And worship God.

Chapter One

THE GOSPEL DEEPS

"The things of the gospel are depths."[1]
—Thomas Goodwin

On the face of it, the good news of Jesus Christ is simply one thing. It is the news—not advice, instruction, or practical steps—that God saves sinners through the life, death, and resurrection of Jesus Christ. Depending on who we might be sharing this news with, we might want to expand a few of those details, mentioning for instance that all men and women are sinners from birth, that Jesus was God himself incarnate in human flesh, that Jesus was (and is) the Messiah, that his death was a substitutionary sacrifice, or that the resurrection was a literal resurrection of a glorified body from a real death. Or we may want to add details in order to put the gospel announcement into the context of the biblical storyline. But the basic facts are there in that first statement—God saves sinners through the life, death, and resurrection of Jesus Christ—which expresses the simple gospel in a clear and concise way.

This simple gospel is power enough to save the most hardened sinner (which is every sinner). Salvation power is conveyed through the gospel message, and received to accomplish a sinner's justification purely by a person's faith, and Jesus tells us that just a mustard seed–sized bit of faith can move mountains (Matt. 17:20). Because of this, then, we know that it is not the size or strength of the faith that saves, but the truth of the faith, and because of *that*, we know it is not our power that rouses our dead heart to trust Jesus, but the Spirit's power working through the gospel that is being believed. This gospel, Paul says, is the power of salvation for all who believe (Rom. 1:16).

---

[1]Thomas Goodwin, *A Discourse of the Glory of the Gospel* in *The Works of Thomas Goodwin* (Edinburgh, UK: James Nichol, 1862), 4:272.

In 1 Corinthians 15:3–4, Paul expresses the simple gospel message this way:

> For I delivered to you as of first importance what I also received: that Christ died for our sins in accordance with the Scriptures, that he was buried, that he was raised on the third day in accordance with the Scriptures.

Paul goes on to relay more historical detail, telling us that Jesus appeared to Peter and the other disciples, then to a crowd of five hundred, then to the apostles, and so on. But the sum of the gospel message Paul is delivering as "of first importance" is contained in verses 3 and 4: Jesus died for our sins, he was buried, and he rose again on the third day. This is the historic news that is the good news.

Simple, isn't it? But 1 Corinthians 15 is anything but simple. As we progress through it, we see that the effects of the gospel are far-reaching and creation-transforming. That the gospel would empower the all-time forgiveness of a person's sins is enormous in itself, but there's more. The rest begins with Paul's crediting the grace of the gospel for doing his good works (v. 10). Then, Paul says, the resurrection of the glorified Jesus activates the future resurrection of all believers (vv. 21–23). Then, because the gospel of Jesus's life, death, and resurrection essentially declares that he is the Messiah, the gospel's power includes the subjection and destruction of all other powers and authorities (v. 24). Finally, not even death escapes the power of the gospel, because by conquering death and the grave, Jesus kills death and the grave (v. 26).

Clearly the gospel is both simple and complex, elementary and advanced. But all of the advanced stuff won't fit on an end zone sign at the Super Bowl, so John 3:16 works just as well.

I have heard it said that the gospel is shallow enough that it is safe for a toddler to swim in, yet deep enough to drown an elephant. We might also think of it this way: We teach our little ones how to read by first teaching them their ABCs. From there, they may move on to the basic principles of phonics. ABCs and phonics are scaled for little children to grasp the English language. But some people get advanced degrees in linguistics. Same category, different levels. The gospel is like that. The ABCs of the gospel work very well for people at all levels of their faith, including wise old pastors and brilliant theologians, but it's possible to explore the ABCs into their inherent complexity.

Although a small child can learn the basics of the English language, many people will nevertheless tell you that English is not the easiest of languages to learn. In the same way, even the simple gospel can be seen less simply. Suppose we use the template "God saves sinners through the life, death, and resurrection of Jesus Christ." We could go point by point through that simple statement and find depth along the way. God saves sinners through Jesus's life? How so? Suddenly we are talking about Christ's active obedience, the tension of the incarnation, the reality of temptation and the reality of sinlessness, and the like. How does God save sinners through Jesus's death? There is a wealth of truth there, and now we are on the verge of discussing the various theories of the atonement. And since the resurrection changes everything, we are ready to talk about everything when we get to it! What sort of salvation does Jesus's resurrection enact for sinners?

What we are glimpsing now is how a wardrobe can contain a world.

When Jesus came, we got all of him. Not a bit of him was held back from us. John 1:16 says that what we get in the gospel is delivered from Jesus's fullness.

The great practical help of this truth is that no matter the day, the circumstance, the sin, or the trouble, there is a grace in the gospel demonstrating God's love for us and empowering us to glorify him. From his fullness, John 1:16 tells us, we receive grace upon grace. In the gospel there is grace for every need, because it comes through an all-sufficient Savior who is the God of steadfast love.

THE DEEP, DEEP LOVE OF GOD

We are in love with God's love. Even non-Christians admire this crucial tenet of the Christian faith, and hardly an atheist exists who does not know both that Jesus commanded us to love our neighbors (Matt. 22:39) and our enemies (Matt. 5:44) and that God is in fact love (1 John 4:8). The weddings of thousands of unbelievers every year will include the so-called "love chapter," 1 Corinthians 13. Love, we know, is the greatest of the things that remain.

Of course, the love of God is a fantastic place to start in doing gospel theology, which is why one of the first ways we teach the gospel to unbelievers or those immature in the faith is through a simple exposition of John 3:16: "For God so loved the world, that he gave his only Son, that whoever believes in him should not perish but have eternal life." But in all of this admiration, by believers and unbelievers both, it's possible we have loaded into the biblical concept of love our preconceptions and presuppositions. It's possible that in all this celebration of God's love, we actually distort the full biblical picture of the love of God.

How great is the love of God? Very, very great. The Scriptures tell us that God's love is steadfast, enduring, unceasing, separation-defying, everlasting to everlasting, and manifested in the inscrutable incarnation. We are told that God's love controls us (2 Cor. 5:14), roots and grounds us (Eph. 3:17), and surpasses knowledge (Eph. 3:19). This is not the kind of love that can be easily captured in religious sentimentalism or humanistic altruism or even romantic emotionalism. This is a specific, personal love that accomplishes things—like saving sinners (Rom. 5:8), disciplining them (Heb. 12:6), and directing their paths (Ps. 25:10)—not a vague, ethereal, "love" that "makes the world go 'round." When the Beatles sing "All you need is love," everyone sings along in agreement, but not everyone knows that while God is love, love is not God.

In fact, one of the chief ways we distort the biblical picture of God's love is when we presuppose, as many Christians do, that love demands freedom. Where we get this notion, I do not know, but it is not in the Bible. In fact, we find in the Bible quite the opposite: the love of God violates human freedoms constantly and consistently. If there's one thing any biblical figure can count on, besides that God loves him, it is that he is not in control of his own destiny. The biblical picture of God's love is bigger, stranger, and more complex than our misguided attempts to assist the gospel by anthropomorphizing God's love. "What the Bible says about the love of God is more complex and nuanced than what is allowed by mere sloganeering," D. A. Carson reminds us.[2]

Some end up sloganeering under the guise of finally doing justice to God's love. The fashionable new waves of postmortem free will, universalism, and inclusivism allege that their views of the love of God are more reflective of the enormity depicted in the Scriptures. Instead, by carrying in philosophical presuppositions about what love must entail in order to be real love, and by seeking to commend the gospel by making this love appear as acceptable to as many people as possible, they take what is multidimensional and squash it out, in effect *flattening* the idea of God's love like pizza dough in a pan in order to make it look bigger.

But the bigness and depth of God's love aren't captured in flatness. They are captured in something more complex, fuller.

What every believer in every age is challenged to do is resist the innate compulsion to flatten out the expansive love of God. Does love demand freedom?

Does love demand giving the loved what he or she wants? The new inclusivists insist yes, and while their desire to maintain the biblical teachings on hell are admirable, we do not find much in the Scriptures to support the idea that, *à la* Lewis, the doors there are locked from the inside. The sentimental tail wags the theological dog when we say that love demands freedom, and that therefore when God consigns the unrepentant to judgment he says, "Thy will be done" to them. In one sense, he *is* saying this, of course, but in the most crucial sense, he is not. In that most crucial sense, when God consigns the ultimately unrepentant to eternal conscious torment, he is saying, "*My* will be done."

What we are asked to believe is that God doing whatever he wants with whomever he wants is a simplistic, fatalistic view of love, and that God letting us do whatever *we* want is a more compelling vision of his love.

No. If my daughter is unaware of the Mack truck bearing down on her, or if she is aware that putting her finger in a light socket

---

[2] D. A. Carson, *The Difficult Doctrine of the Love of God* (Wheaton, IL: Crossway, 2000), 24.

will electrocute her but she wants to do it anyway, do I love her if I am able to intervene but defer to her freedom? Or am I a loving father to tackle her out of the truck's way, to slap her hand away from the socket?

"Ah," but some will say, "God lets children get hit by Mack trucks and electrocuted by light sockets every day." Yes, he does. And so already we are faced with what to do with this information as it relates to "God is love."

Since God loves everyone, perhaps "God is love" means he will some day tackle everyone, including the unrepentant and spiritually dead haters of God, out of the way of eternal death. Because the only other alternative, on this train of thought, is to believe that God does *not* in fact love everyone.

Or maybe the reality is a love more multifaceted than we can understand with finite, fallen minds. Maybe the reality is that the God of the Bible is as transcendent as he is immanent, that his ways are inscrutable, that his love is glorious and astonishing precisely because it is too wonderful for us. Maybe the heights and breadths of God's love do not refer merely to its size but also to its complexity.

In Trevor Francis's great hymn "O the Deep, Deep Love of Jesus," we sing:

> O the deep, deep love of Jesus, vast, unmeasured, boundless, free!
> Rolling as a mighty ocean in its fullness over me!
> Underneath me, all around me, is the current of Thy love
> Leading onward, leading homeward to Thy glorious rest above!

In Walter Matheson's hymn "O Love That Will Not Let Me Go," we sing of the "ocean depths" of God's love. Francis and Matheson give us a more fitting symbol for the biblical picture of God's love. It is deep like the ocean, and not just in fathoms and leagues, but in diversity and complexity. There are clear shallows to play in and opaque depths of mystery. There are hidden places in the ocean, places we will never see, places too deep for us to go. There are things about the ocean depths small children can understand, things marine biologists still haven't figured out, and things nobody will ever discover to even have the opportunity to scrutinize. As Augustine is thought to have said, "I have seen the depths, but I cannot find the bottom."

And then, since we are alleged people of the Book, we know that the unfathomable ocean of God's love does not exist in a vacuum, hermetically sealed off from all the other "things" God is and God does. He does not say "Jacob have I loved, Esau have I also loved." And while "hated" in that instance (Mal. 1:2–3; Rom. 9:13) may not mirror the sort of hatred we are most familiar with today, this point is itself a good reminder that neither does "love" in that instance take its cue from our conception of it. The Bible shows us our God, who is love, saying and doing all sorts of things most of our more sensitive souls would not consider loving at all. We must remember, then, that God's oceanic love occupies space in the perfect balance of the infinite universe of all his attributes. He is love, yes, but he is also just and jealous. Richard Lovelace concurs, writing in his classic work *Dynamics of Spiritual Life*:

> God's mercy, patience and love must be fully preached in the church. But they are not *credible* unless they are presented in tension with God's infinite power, complete and sovereign control of the universe, holiness, and righteousness. And where God's righteousness is clearly presented, compassionate warnings of his holy anger against sin must be given, and warnings also of the certainty of divine judgment in endless alienation from God which will be unimaginably worse than the literal descriptions of hell. It is no wonder that the world and the church are not awakened when our leadership is either singing a lullaby concerning these matters or presenting them in a caricature which is so grotesque that it is unbelievable.
>
> The tension between God's holy righteousness and his compassionate mercy cannot be legitimately resolved by remolding his character into an image of pure benevolence as the church did in the nineteenth century.[3]

It is a sad irony, then, that the ever-fashionable impulse to do

---

[3] Richard Lovelace, *Dynamics of Spiritual Life: An Evangelical Theology of Renewal* (Downer's Grove, IL: InterVarsity, 1979), 84–85.

justice to the depths of God's love amounts to a very dramatic exercise in one-dimensionalism. God's love is polyhedronal stuff. Woe to the flatteners of what is hyperspatial, multidimensional, intra-Trinitarian, and eternal in ways awesomer than "one year after another."

We can feel the weight of this complicated awesomeness in Paul's prayer in Ephesians 3:14–19:

> For this reason I bow my knees before the Father, from whom every family in heaven and on earth is named, that according to the riches of his glory he may grant you to be strengthened with power through his Spirit in your inner being, so that Christ may dwell in your hearts through faith—that you, being rooted and grounded in love, may have strength to comprehend with all the saints what is the breadth and length and height and depth, and to know the love of Christ that surpasses knowledge, that you may be filled with all the fullness of God.

We may know a love that is beyond our knowing. (We are given the amount we need in the cross of Christ, itself a comprehensible prelude to incomprehensible "subsequent glories.") But we will need the strength of Spiritual[4] power in our insidest insides to scratch the surface of this comprehension. We won't even come close with our clichés and sentimentality.

God's love is much deeper than that. It is more fascinating than that. The angels certainly find it so:

> Concerning this salvation, the prophets who prophesied about the grace that was to be yours searched and inquired carefully, inquiring what person or time the Spirit of Christ in them was indicating when he predicted the sufferings of Christ and the subsequent glories. It was revealed to them that they were serving not themselves but you, in the things that have now been announced to you through those who preached the good news to you by the Holy Spirit sent from heaven, things into which angels long to look. (1 Pet. 1:10–12)

---

[4] I capitalize the word "Spiritual" when I mean to differentiate between the work of the Holy Spirit and generically "religious" activity.

I love Peter's phrase "subsequent glories" in this passage. The atoning work of Christ unleashes a beautiful torrent of goodness, like a Pandora's Box of blessings. In 2 Peter 1:4, he tells us that through knowledge of Christ's glory and excellence, we have received "precious and very great promises," *plural*.

The gospel's content—Jesus's sinless life, sacrificial death, and bodily resurrection—is deep and multifaceted, but so are the implications and accomplishments of the content. Through the historical work of the gospel, future blessings pour out and stream in abundance. Paul reflects this when he speaks of the gospel this way: "In the whole world it is bearing fruit and increasing" (Col. 1:5–6). As the whole tree is in the acorn, then, so blossoming glories are in the gospel of "Christ crucified."

But the cross and the empty tomb are not tantamount to an acorn (or an English garden). They are a supernova. And in the gospel there are supernovas within supernovas. Or we may say that the gospel is a diamond—it is one precious jewel, but it is one precious jewel with many different facets, each with a brilliance and vision of its own.

Because the love of God is deep, we should expect that the gospel it births is deep, as well. We will be looking at some of the facets of the gospel and its implications throughout this book, but as a sort of "gospel depth primer," here are five primary ways in which the gospel of Jesus Christ is deep.

THE GOSPEL'S WORK IS BOTH PERSONAL AND COSMIC

Many of us are accustomed to presenting the gospel as a personal transaction between an individual sinner and God, inviting those who receive our witness to "accept Jesus" as their "personal Lord and Savior." This is not an entirely wrong approach to gospel witness, I think, but it can be difficult to find in the general mode of Jesus's preaching and teaching. He clearly tells individuals that they are forgiven, that they must be born again, that they ought to go and sin no more, but the grander scope of Jesus's witness testifies to something larger than personal salvation of individual sinners.

We cannot and should not say that the gospel is less than the personal salvation of individual sinners, but it is certainly *more* than that.

John the Baptist prefaces Jesus's arrival by announcing that the kingdom is "at hand." As Jesus conducts his earthly ministry, Matthew's Gospel tells us, he and his disciples are heralding "the gospel of the kingdom." Throughout the chronicle of this ministry we see Jesus performing miracles and teaching in parables. What exactly is he doing? He is testifying to the good news that God's kingdom is coming to bear in and through himself, that God's will is beginning to be done on earth as it is in heaven because the true King has now arrived and is getting to business setting things back to rights. One of the first things Jesus does in his public ministry is announce the fulfillment of Isaiah's prophecy of the year of the Lord's favor:

> And he came to Nazareth, where he had been brought up. And as was his custom, he went to the synagogue on the Sabbath day, and he stood up to read. And the scroll of the prophet Isaiah was given to him. He unrolled the scroll and found the place where it was written,
>
> > "The Spirit of the Lord is upon me,
> >   because he has anointed me
> >   to proclaim good news to the poor.
> > He has sent me to proclaim liberty to the captives
> >   and recovering of sight to the blind,
> >   to set at liberty those who are oppressed,
> > to proclaim the year of the Lord's favor."
>
> And he rolled up the scroll and gave it back to the attendant and sat down. And the eyes of all in the synagogue were fixed on him. And he began to say to them, "Today this Scripture has been fulfilled in your hearing." (Luke 4:16–21)

Jesus is reading from what we know today as Isaiah 61, the fourth verse of which reads:

They shall build up the ancient ruins;
    they shall raise up the former devastations;
they shall repair the ruined cities,
    the devastations of many generations.

Jesus reads this prophecy with himself at the center, then orients his entire ministry around the restoration of these ancient ruins and former devastations. He is God's justice come to life and brought to bear. All that he does in this effort leads directly to the cross and the tomb, upon which everything hinges, but all of this ministry is squarely aimed at the restoration of all things. Habakkuk 2:14 projects God's purposes as the filling of the whole earth with the knowledge of God's glory as the waters cover the sea; Paul tells us that "all things" will be placed in subjection to Christ (1 Cor. 15:27–28; Phil. 3:21); and Revelation 21:23 looks to the day when the holy city of the new heavens and the new earth has no need for a sun because the Lamb himself will be its lamp. Obviously what God is going for in sending the Son to live, die, and rise again is an all-encompassing restoration and purification, of which my accepting Jesus as my personal Lord and Savior is (no doubt) a part, but not the whole.

This world is fallen. It is fallen because we are fallen. We caused the problem and we are the chief problem *in* the problem, but our problem is so problematic, it caused multiple problems. Romans 8:19–22 makes this connection explicit for us:

> For the creation waits with eager longing for the revealing of the sons of God. For the creation was subjected to futility, not willingly, but because of him who subjected it, in hope that the creation itself will be set free from its bondage to corruption and obtain the freedom of the glory of the children of God. For we know that the whole creation has been groaning together in the pains of childbirth until now.

Why is creation so messed up? Is it bad? Certainly not. But we are, and we are so bad that our badness has ramifications bigger and wider than ourselves. We see this consequence in the curse of the fall.

To Adam he said,

> "Because you have listened to the voice of your wife
>> and have eaten of the tree
> of which I commanded you,
>> 'You shall not eat of it,'
> cursed is the ground because of you;
>> in pain you shall eat of it all the days of your life;
> thorns and thistles it shall bring forth for you;
>> and you shall eat the plants of the field.
> By the sweat of your face
>> you shall eat bread,
> till you return to the ground,
>> for out of it you were taken;
> for you are dust,
>> and to dust you shall return."

. . . Therefore the LORD God sent him out from the garden of Eden to work the ground from which he was taken. (Gen. 3:17–19, 23)

To demonstrate the severity of disobedience, God cursed the very creation he'd given Adam and Eve to take dominion over. The harmony broken between man and God leads to disharmony everywhere, in every phase and sphere of life. All creation is groaning now, which means our sin doesn't have just personal, relational consequences; it has cosmic, spiritual consequences as well.

So the gospel that Jesus preaches in his earthly ministry inaugurates the kingdom of God by announcing that he is at work to reverse this entire curse! By declaring his own sinless kingship, he is proclaiming that he will personally redeem what Adam (and we) personally cursed. By casting out demons, he is demonstrating that the spiritual forces of wickedness that reign over the cursed earth are being overthrown and conquered. By performing miracles, he is providing signposts to the kingdom's consummation, offering glimpses of the day in the age to come when there will be no sickness, no death, no deformity, and no lack. By teaching in parables, he is showing snapshots of what redeemed life inside the kingdom looks like.

By going to the cross, he offers himself as the propitiating sacrifice for the sin that caused all of the breakdown to begin with. By rising from the grave, he presents the firstfruits of the kingdom's consummation.

The big picture of all that Jesus has done and is doing, then, encompasses our personal forgiveness and eternal relationship with God but is scaled larger to fit the scope of the restoration of a fallen creation. So if all you've heard about being saved is that it's about going to heaven when you die, you have really heard a truncated gospel. That is part of being saved. But being saved is really all about God setting us apart to fit the future connection between heaven and earth in the age to come. This is the fullness of what the gospel is all about. This is why the suffering Job's hope is not disembodied bliss in heaven but seeing God "in his flesh" and seeing his redeemer standing "on the earth" (Job 19:25–26).

You may be familiar with the two shorthand ways many pastors and writers express the narrative of the gospel. Some outline the gospel story this way:

God—Man—Christ—Response

We would flesh out that expression to say that a holy God created mankind, mankind disobeyed and thereby brought separation between himself and God, but Christ came in the love of God to pay the penalty of sin and rise again from the grave to purchase the hope of eternal life, and that now man must respond in faith to receive Christ's work and be forgiven and reconciled.

Others will outline the gospel story this way:

Creation—Fall—Redemption—Restoration

We might flesh out that outline to say that God created the world, and man for it, all good and perfect, but that when man disobeyed, he brought about the wide-ranging fall of the world, and man in it, but that in Christ's atoning work, God's plan is to restore what is fallen, all to be consummated in the new heavens and new earth ushered in at the future return of Jesus.

Is the first expression of the gospel the right way, or is the second the right way? The answer is *yes*.

So long as both narratives are hinging upon the atoning work of the sinless Christ on the cross and out of the tomb, they are both biblically faithful expressions of the gospel. We might say that the first expression shows us the personal gospel and the second shows us the cosmic gospel. Matt Chandler calls the first expression "The Gospel on the Ground" because it presents the microlevel view of Jesus's saving work, and he calls the second expression "The Gospel in the Air" because it presents the macrolevel view.[5] We could say the first expression is the gospel through a microscope and the second is the gospel through a telescope.

In any event, what the Bible shows us is that God saves sinners through the life, death, and resurrection of Jesus Christ, and this salvation is the primary and central piece of the whole redemptive puzzle, the big picture of which reveals that God is saving the world through the life, death, and resurrection of Jesus Christ. (We will explore this concept a bit further in chapter 2's discussion of a "redemptive place" and more fully in chapter 9, on the cosmic redemption.)

There is another depth to the gospel, however.

THE GOSPEL PRESENTS THE FULLNESS OF GOD

What the Scriptures show us about the gospel's design and the gospel's power is that it is the result of the entirety of the godhead. To put it another way, in the gospel, all divine hands are on deck!

Peter even introduces himself by commending the particular work of the Father, the Son, and the Holy Spirit in the gospel that has made his recipients "elect exiles":

> Peter, an apostle of Jesus Christ, To those who are elect exiles of the Dispersion in Pontus, Galatia, Cappadocia, Asia, and Bithynia, according to the foreknowledge of God the Father, in the sancti-

---

[5] Matt Chandler, *The Explicit Gospel* (Wheaton, IL: Crossway, 2012).

fication of the Spirit, for obedience to Jesus Christ and for sprinkling with his blood: May grace and peace be multiplied to you.
(1 Pet. 1:1–2)

What Peter has revealed to us in just a simple, concise intro-
duction is an enormous depth to the gospel, a depth reflective of
the depths of God himself. By identifying his believing recipients
as "elect . . . according to the foreknowledge of God the Father," he
locates the gospel's genesis in the atemporal love and sovereignty of
God (a concept we will explore a bit further in chap. 7). By identifying these believers as "elect . . . in the sanctification of the Spirit,"
he highlights the unique work of the Spirit in the gospel of regen-
erating hearts, stirring senses, and opening ears and eyes to comprehend and treasure Christ's work. By identifying these believers
as "elect . . . for obedience to Jesus Christ and for sprinkling with
his blood," Peter identifies the effective work *in* the gospel—Christ's
atoning sacrifice—and the effective work *of* the gospel—our con-
formity to the image of Jesus in glorifying God by our obedience
to him.

Peter is just saying hello. But he has essentially revealed what
Fred Sanders would call "the Trinitarian contour"[6] of the gospel. Sanders writes, "The gospel is Trinitarian, and the Trinity is
the gospel. Christian salvation comes from the Trinity, happens
through the Trinity, and brings us home to the Trinity."[7]

We see a hint of this contour in the "golden chain" of Romans
8:30: "And those whom he predestined he also called, and those
whom he called he also justified, and those whom he justified
he also glorified." As we see the Scripture's unfolding revelation
of these events, we know that God the Father predestines us, the
Spirit effectually calls us, and the Son's work justifies and glorifies
us. But of course the Spirit applies this justifying and glorifying
work to us at the Father's discretion.

What we are seeing is that not a bit of God's God-ness is held
back from doing what must be done to forgive our sins and cleanse

---

[6] Fred Sanders, *The Deep Things of God: How the Trinity Changes Everything* (Wheaton, IL: Crossway, 2010), 100.
[7] Ibid., 10.

us from all unrighteousness. He is not stingy with himself, and in fact is willing to dazzle us with just how hands-on he is. Quoth Sanders: "The blessing of the gospel, in other words, is big and God-shaped."[8]

We will explore this depth more extensively in chapter 3 on the Trinitarian gospel, but suffice it to say that while God does not grow weary in doing all the things that are impossible for us to do, he certainly does *a lot* of work with this good news.

THE GOSPEL RECONCILES US ON MULTIPLE LEVELS

"The sum of the gospel embassy is to reconcile us to God," Calvin writes.[9]

Reconciliation of sinners to a holy God is the essence of what the gospel *does*:

> For if while we were enemies we were reconciled to God by the death of his Son, much more, now that we are reconciled, shall we be saved by his life. More than that, we also rejoice in God through our Lord Jesus Christ, through whom we have now received reconciliation. (Rom. 5:10–11)

Because God is holy and we are not, we are at odds with each other. We are rebels against God, deniers of his sovereign Lordship, and worshipers of ourselves. Paul's language in Ephesians 2:1–3 piles on about our despicability: apart from Christ, he tells us, we are dead, we are Satan-worshipers, we are lustful appetite-followers, and we are objects of wrath. I'm not sure how we could get much worse than that.

But I know how we can get better! "But God, being rich in mercy, because of the great love with which he loved us, even when we were dead in our trespasses, made us alive together with Christ—by grace you have been saved" (Eph. 2:4–5).

There are at least three levels in the reconciling work of Christ.

1. *The gospel reconciles individuals to God.* In this first level we see that by believing in Jesus's atoning work and thereby receiving

---

[8] Ibid., 100.
[9] John Calvin, *Institutes of the Christian Religion*, ed. John T. McNeill, trans. Ford Lewis Battles, 2 vols. (Philadelphia: Westminster, 1960), 1:729.

forgiveness through faith in him, we are reconciled as individuals to God the Father. The parable of the prodigal son is perhaps the most recognizable illustration of this reconciliation.

Jesus lives the sinless life we could not, absorbs the wrath we deserve in dying the death we owe, and rises again the third day that we might rise in the day to come. This work makes atonement and secures our position in the heavenly places with Jesus (Eph. 2:6). We who are far from God are brought near by the gospel. We have now received reconciliation. Paul writes, "All this is from God, who through Christ reconciled us to himself " (2 Cor. 5:18).

2. *The gospel reconciles individuals to each other.* We see in the curse of the fall not just enmity between man and beast, and not just enmity between man and God because of man's sin, but a very real enmity between the man and the woman. There is a division now between human relationships; they too are stained by our disobedience and fractured because of our self-interest, self-centeredness, and self-exaltation. In Genesis 3, as God is confronting the newly dead sinners, both Adam and Eve pass the buck. Adam blames Eve and Eve blames the serpent. Neither is repentant, and so both establish the pattern of relational dysfunction that will plague all of society until Christ returns and makes his society the only society.

Of course, Adam and Eve's primary sin is sin against God. Their sin against each other is merely the rotten fruit of falling short of God's glory. But the rotten fruit is here nonetheless. As part of the curse, God says, "Your desire shall be for your husband, and he shall rule over you" (Gen. 3:16). This is not the good desire and good rule of grace-based biblical marriage; this is selfish exploitation of each other, a consequence that hits all personal relationships as a reflection of the broken relationship.

The Law provides a compensating template for God's aim for relationships. In the Ten Commandments we see how the first table of commands corresponds to our vertical relationship with God—having no other gods before him, not making any idols, not taking his name in vain, and keeping the Sabbath—while the second table corresponds to our horizontal relationships with others—not stealing from them or killing them, for example.

Of course, the horizontal relationship commands are directly connected to the vertical relationship commands. In fact, if I steal from you, it's because I have had another god before God. But even this truth demonstrates how integrally connected the gospel of Jesus Christ is to the way we treat each other; if I am centered on the gospel, my Lord is Jesus, and if my Lord is Jesus, I don't want your wife or your stuff. If my Lord is Jesus, I want the best for you and want to demonstrate that by loving you. ("By this all people will know that you are my disciples, if you have love for one another," John 13:35.)

Jesus himself makes the connection when he's asked to name the greatest commandment. "And he said to him, 'You shall love the Lord your God with all your heart and with all your soul and with all your mind. This is the great and first commandment. And a second is like it: You shall love your neighbor as yourself'" (Matt. 22:37–39). Jesus explicitly connects love for God with love for neighbor, which is a reflection of the two tables of the Ten Commandments and a reflection of how the gospel that reconciles us to the Father then reconciles us to each other.

Paul makes this connection, as well, when he writes about how being reconciled to God gives us the ministry of reconciliation (2 Cor. 5:18–19), but Paul's reconciliatory aims are bigger than just you and me playing nice.

3. *The gospel reconciles us together to God.* The gospel reconciles us as individuals to God, and it reconciles us as individuals to each other, but God's plan in this reconciling work is bigger and broader than even those blessed effects. God is not just concerned with making us different people but making us *a* people. What I mean is, it is not just that God wants you and me to be kind and gentle and forgiving and obedient; he wants us to be kind and gentle and forgiving and obedient *together*, because the plan he has designed to most display his glory in the reflected image of his Son is not saved individuals but a saved church. Paul puts it this way:

> So then you are no longer strangers and aliens, but you are fellow
> citizens with the saints and members of the household of God,

built on the foundation of the apostles and prophets, Christ Jesus himself being the cornerstone, in whom the whole structure, being joined together, grows into a holy temple in the Lord. In him you also are being built together into a dwelling place for God by the Spirit. (Eph. 2:19–22)

We are being sanctified as individuals, to be sure, but part of this sanctifying work of the Spirit is the reconciliation of ourselves to each other, which is an effect of the Spirit's reconciling us together to God as the spotless bride of Jesus Christ. We "are being built together" into a unified temple, a household of God. As Christians we reflect a "little Christ"-ness, but as the church we reflect the body of Christ.

We will explore the complex reconciling work of the gospel a bit more in chapter 8, but it is enough to say now that denying any of these three levels of gospel reconciliation—individuals to God, individuals to each other, us together to God—is selling the gospel short.

THE GOSPEL SAVES US TOTALLY

How else is the gospel deep? If John 1:16 is true, we know that we receive "grace upon grace" from the fullness of Jesus. This means there is an endless supply of grace. There is enough for our every need (Phil. 4:19; Heb. 4:16)

If the gospel is not the ABCs of the Christian life but the A to Z, we can expect that the gospel is for all of life, not just the moment of conversion. The gospel's saving work is deep work. It is deep tissue massage, spiritual reparative therapy, and radical reconstructive surgery.

The gospel forgives our sins once for all. It gives us a new identity. It secures us citizenship in heaven and the hope of eternal life. Once believed, it is the grounds of our justification; thereafter believed, it is the power of our sanctification; finally believed, it results in our glorification. If we believe in the gospel, we are saved from the curse of the law, the condemnation of wrath, and the consequence of hell. If we believe in the gospel, we receive all that Jesus is for all that we are. All of this comes from what Christ has done.

Hebrews 7:25 tells us, "Consequently, he is able to save to the uttermost those who draw near to God through him, since he always lives to make intercession for them." The author of Hebrews makes it a point to let us know that while the old covenant required repeated sacrifices for repeated sins, the new covenant is a better one because Jesus is its guarantor (7:22), and he has offered himself as a sacrifice once for all (7:27).

God promises in the gospel to begin a work in us and then to finish it. And we will be as saved as Christ's atoning work was perfect, which is to say *totally*.

THE GOSPEL REFLECTS THE MULTIPLE EXCELLENCIES OF CHRIST

Take a look at these short verses on the nature of Jesus:

> To them God chose to make known how great among the Gentiles are the riches of the glory of this mystery, which is Christ in you, the hope of glory. (Col. 1:27)

> To me, though I am the very least of all the saints, this grace was given, to preach to the Gentiles the unsearchable riches of Christ. (Eph. 3:8)

> He is the radiance of the glory of God and the exact imprint of his nature, and he upholds the universe by the word of his power. (Heb. 1:3)

Riches. *Unsearchable* riches. Radiance. Glory. Truly we have a deep, deep Savior.

The writers of Scripture pile on the adjectives and superlatives to help us glimpse Jesus's all-surpassing awesomeness. We have in the Bible the perfect communication from God himself, but even these perfect descriptors hint at more and more beyond themselves, levels of greatness so staggering they could not be captured adequately in words but only hinted at in awe-struck circumlocutions, as if hiding in rhetorical crevasses to merely peek at the backside of God's glory.

We are told that his riches are unsearchable, that his power is surpassing (2 Cor. 4:7). Even John has to stop at some point, because it would not be possible to say too much: "Now there are also many other things that Jesus did. Were every one of them to be written, I suppose that the world itself could not contain the books that would be written" (John 21:25).

Before Abraham was, Jesus is. He was in the beginning with God and was God and through him God created the world. He was the mystery visitation angel of the patriarchs. He was slain from the foundation of the world. He is the King. He is the Way, the Truth, and the Life. He is the Vine. He is the Door. He is the Light. He is the Alpha and the Omega, the First and the Last. He is our Advocate, our Intercessor, our Guarantor.

John Calvin writes, "Christ is, as it were, a fountain, open to us, from which we may draw what otherwise would lie unprofitably hidden in that deep and secret spring."[10]

This is the Jesus whose gospel we receive, and this is the Jesus we receive in the gospel!

When some friends and I were once leading a church's young adult ministry, we were called to a meeting with our pastor. He was relatively new to the church and was getting to know the ministry leaders, and this meeting was especially important as we had some internal conflicts on our team regarding the focus of our ministry.

"What is it you want this ministry to offer?" the pastor asked us.

My coleader, who is really the guy who founded the ministry as a Bible study in his living room, explained how he had begun by trying to respond to a need he discerned among college students and young adults to "go deeper."

The pastor kinda-sorta flinched. Like many men in his position, he had heard this phrase plenty of times, usually as a part of criticism of his preaching or teaching. The underlying assertion is that what we normally receive at church is shallow or superficial. I have since heard and read plenty of pastors complain in their sermons or on their blogs about people in their church who want deeper teaching. These folks are usually derided and accused of

---

[10] Ibid., 1:736.

being consumeristic babies or legalistic eggheads. Certainly some of those types have made this complaint.

The problem is that we think we know what deep is. We think "going deep" means studying the end times or the Calvinism/ Arminianism debate. We think that deeper teaching means less application or more application. We think it means digging into the original languages and getting at the root of the root of the root.[11]

"What does 'deep' mean?" our pastor asked me. I was the ministry's teacher, after all.

I said, "Deep means Jesus."

I am afraid there weren't many in the room who understood that, even after I explained that every teaching ought to center on or highlight Jesus, and that this could never get old or stale because Jesus can't be boring. There's too much of him. And not only is Jesus the person we're supposed to be most interested in, he happens to be the most interesting person in the universe anyway.

I will do my best to bask in Jesus's multitudinous glories in chapter 10, but the working thesis of this entire book is that the gospel is deep with grace abounding because Jesus is deep with grace abounding. This good news reflects the person and work of the One who is good—Christ, who is as perfect as he is complex, full as he is eternal, beautiful as he is omnipotent.

---

[11] I highly recommend D. A. Carson's *Exegetical Fallacies* (Grand Rapids, MI: Baker, 1996) for the guardrails it provides for this kind of thinking.

Chapter Two

THE GOSPEL'S THREEFOLD VISION

"Oh, Jesus rose from the dead
Come on, get out of your bed."
—Keith Green[1]

The church in the West is sleepwalking. Why? We don't lack for dynamic preachers, innovative church models, entrepreneurial spirit, wealthy benefactors, high technology, or widespread media and cultural saturation. Yet while the biggest churches get bigger, the number of Christians in America is shrinking, and even in those big churches, leaders are discovering a discipleship deficit of emergency proportions.

I am not an expert in missiology or ecclesiology or sociology, but I can read what the Bible says. In its pages I read that the source of the church's power is the Holy Spirit working through the proclamation of the gospel of Jesus Christ. No other source is credited with transforming power, not even intelligence or good works, much less creativity and good marketing. Uneducated men with stuttering tongues and unclever speech set the world on fire because they were content to simply arrange the wood and trust the torch of the gospel to do its thing.

What we are left to deduce is that either we are faithful to gospel-centered ministry but God doesn't work that way any-more—in which case the Bible's claim that the gospel is power needs a retroactive expiration date—or else our half-hearted, defeated, apathetic Christianity is a result of our gospel-deficient Christianity.

What can wake us up? A better vision. The gospel does not

---

[1] Keith Green, "Asleep in the Light," *No Compromise* (Sparrow Records, 1990).

merely give us a ticket to heaven, a lifeline to stuff in our pocket for safekeeping—it gives us a new worldview. It gives us eyes to see and ears to hear; it expands our vision to behold the vistas of eternity and deepens our vision to see the world through redemption-colored glasses.

Isaiah was undone by the vision of God's glory in the temple. Paul was hijacked by a blinding light. Peter was shaken by the descending linen. The disciples fell on their faces during Christ's transfiguration.

None of them was unchanged by what they saw, and while none of them followed God perfectly after their vision, they certainly saw God, themselves, and the world differently even after the vision had faded.

When John the Baptist began preparing the way for Jesus's entry into public ministry, he cried out in the words of Isaiah 40:3–5:

> A voice cries:
> "In the wilderness prepare the way of the LORD;
>   make straight in the desert a highway for our God.
> Every valley shall be lifted up,
>   and every mountain and hill be made low;
> the uneven ground shall become level,
>   and the rough places a plain.
> And the glory of the LORD shall be revealed,
>   and all flesh shall see it together,
>   for the mouth of the LORD has spoken."

What a beautiful cataclysm this foretells! When the king comes, his arrival is earth-shaking. The gospel changes the landscape.

When we behold the gospel's bigness, we behold the true bigness of everything else. There are three primary things the gospel expands our vision of, and I see them embedded in these words of Peter:

> But you are a chosen race, a royal priesthood, a holy nation, a people for his own possession, that you may proclaim the excel-

lencies of him who called you out of darkness into his marvelous light. (1 Pet. 2:9)

Peter is admonishing the church to abstain from fleshly talk and actions, to obey diligently in order to commend the gospel and reflect the holiness of God. It is as if he's saying in 1 Peter 2:9, "Besides, don't you know who you are?" And his declaration of who they/we are evinces the gospel's threefold vision.

THE GOSPEL GIVES US A SECURE VIEW OF SELF

Many Christians' problems of fear, doubt, and complacency stem from forgetting who they are, which is to say, who they are *in Christ*. Paul is quite clear: "Therefore, if anyone is in Christ, he is a new creation. The old has passed away; behold, the new has come" (2 Cor. 5:17). It is true that we are simultaneously sinners and saints, but when we are not operating according to the gospel's resurrection power, it is because we believe that greater is the world than he that is within us.

Even the Christian with his nose to the obedience grindstone can miss out on this transforming positional view. I may outwardly look very diligent in the faith and dutiful in good works, good words, and good manners, but if inwardly that is all the result of an insecurity about my standing with God, the hardest work I can muster will be both worry-inducing and worthless. The performance treadmill simply leads to exhaustion.

But the gospel says I am free from the curse of the law, which means I am free from the burden of the law's demands. Christ has met them for me. Christ's righteousness is credited to my account. Christ hides me within himself. If all this is true, I am as secure as Christ is.

God's affection does not have to be earned; in fact, it *can't* be earned (by us, anyway). God's affection is freely given. When we really grasp that the gospel is saying this about God and about ourselves, our sense of identity will blossom, swell, and strengthen.

Look again at how 1 Peter 2:9 describes our position, thanks to the gospel of Jesus.

A CHOSEN RACE

This means that God *picked* us. In the days of my youth in Houston, Texas, I played pick-up basketball or football with my buddies nearly every weekend at our favorite park. When it came time to form teams, I enjoyed very often being the first or second pick. I had serious game, I assure you. Then my wife and I moved to Nashville, Tennessee. I stopped playing sports every weekend. Several years later on a visit back home, the old gang decided to get together to throw the pigskin around. We began to form teams, and even though I had given no more demonstration of my current fitness level than simply walking from the car to the field, I was picked second to last. Oh, how the mighty had fallen! I was humiliated. All these guys had done was look at me; I guess several years had taken the sheen off their memories of my athletic prowess. I suddenly looked less Tom Brady and more Tom Bosley.

I felt very keenly in that moment how good it feels to be picked. Everybody wants to be picked.

The gospel tells an interesting story about being picked. If I had to relate it to my weekend football humiliation, I would put it this way: God looks at the available selection, sees that I have no evident talent or ability and that in fact I give all indications of being a liability to the team, not an asset, and says, "I'll take him first."

He does this for all of us. He picks us. Not because we're great players, but because Jesus is. We can contribute nothing to God; he is not needful of us. There's nothing that he can't get done without us. But there he goes, picking us. And he purposefully picks the scrubs, the benchwarmers, the C team. In God's economy, he chooses the last to be first, blesses the poor in spirit with riches aplenty, and exalts the humble.

You thought this whole deal was your idea? Nope. "You did not choose me, but I chose you" (John 15:16). You think you were picked based on your ability? Nope. "So then it depends not on human will or exertion, but on God, who has mercy" (Rom. 9:16). You think you were picked when you entered the draft? Nope. "He chose us in him before the foundation of the world" (Eph. 1:4).

A ROYAL PRIESTHOOD

God doesn't just take the scrubs; he takes the scrubs and turns them into frontline warriors. He makes the C team the A team. He raises our estate. He makes us not serfs in the kingdom, but brothers and sisters of the King, princes and princesses under his lordship. He has seated us with Christ in the heavenly places (Eph. 2:6); the gospel gives us the royal treatment, and one day we will have the crowns to show for it (James 1:12; 1 Pet. 5:4).

But we aren't just any kind of royalty; we are royal priests. We're made ambassadors for Christ, go-betweens charged by God to bring the ministry of reconciliation to the lost, commissioned to make disciples of the nations. We pour out our lives as Christ did his own, in order that we might testify to the saving sacrifice of him who makes our sacrificial witness a glory to God. In the days of old, we needed priests to make atonement for us. Now that the High Priest has made atonement once for all, we have become priests ourselves, given full access to the throne of grace inside the holy of holies. Indeed, our bodies are now the temples of the Spirit.

Are you catching yet just how much God makes of us? There is more.

A HOLY NATION

When God tells us "You shall be holy, for I am holy," it is a command, but it's also a promise. And because we can't make ourselves perfectly holy, he does it for us. The blood of his Son cleanses us from all unrighteousness. Christ's goodness is set to our account, and we are set apart from the condemnation hanging over the world. We are set apart for special use, consecrated by our saving God whose plans for us include demonstrating the expansiveness of his perfect holiness throughout the world.

A PEOPLE FOR HIS OWN POSSESSION

Put simply, God owns us. Of course, God really owns everybody, but he treats those trusting in his Son as his own children. He treats them differently, specially. He marks them out, covers them, secures their future, and gives them a hope. He sends his Spirit to indwell, convict, teach, and comfort them.

And here's the deal: nobody steals God's stuff. If he owns you, he *owns* you. Those whom Christ has purchased for the Father will not get lost or be forfeited (John 6:39; 10:28).[2]

Jesus cleanses us from all unrighteousness. How are we not staggered by this minute by minute? Look how *saved* we are!

While I do not agree with all of what Neil Anderson has written—particularly as some of his work appears at odds with the concept of *simul justus et peccator*[3]—I greatly appreciate the following list of gospel affirmations he includes in his book *Victory Over the Darkness*, and have used it personally and in counseling:

> Since I am in Christ, by the grace of God . . .
> I have been justified—completely forgiven and made righteous (Rom. 5:1).
> I died with Christ and died to the power of sin's rule over my life (Rom. 6:1–6).
> I am free forever from condemnation (Rom. 8:1).
> I have been placed into Christ by God's doing (1 Cor. 1:30).
> I have received the Spirit of God into my life that I might know the things freely given to me by God (1 Cor. 2:12).
> I have been given the mind of Christ (1 Cor. 2:16).
> I have been bought with a price; I am not my own; I belong to God (1 Cor. 6:19, 20).
> I have been established, anointed and sealed by God in Christ, and I have been given the Holy Spirit as a pledge guaranteeing my inheritance to come (2 Cor. 1:21; Eph. 1:13, 14).
> Since I have died, I no longer live for myself, but for Christ (2 Cor. 5:14, 15).
> I have been made righteous (2 Cor. 5:21).
> I have been crucified with Christ and it is no longer I who live, but Christ who lives in me. The life I am now living is Christ's life (Gal. 2:20).
> I have been blessed with every spiritual blessing (Eph. 1:3).

---

[2] The doctrine of eternal security is explored more fully in chapter 7.
[3] The phrase is Latin, roughly meaning "simultaneously righteous and a sinner." Drawing heavily from Paul's teaching in Romans 7, the idea came to special prominence in the days of the Reformation, primarily in the work of Martin Luther.

I was chosen in Christ before the foundation of the world to be holy and am without blame before Him (Eph. 1:4).

I was predestined—determined by God—to be adopted as God's son (Eph. 1:5).

I have been redeemed and forgiven, and I am a recipient of His lavish grace.

I have been made alive together with Christ (Eph. 2:5).

I have been raised up and seated with Christ in heaven (Eph. 2:6).

I have direct access to God through the Spirit (Eph. 2:18).

I may approach God with boldness, freedom and confidence (Eph. 3:12).

I have been rescued from the domain of Satan's rule and transferred to the kingdom of Christ (Col. 1:13).

I have been redeemed and forgiven of all my sins. The debt against me has been canceled (Col. 1:14).

Christ Himself is in me (Col. 1:27).

I am firmly rooted in Christ and am now being built in Him (Col. 2:7).

I have been spiritually circumcised . . . (Col. 2:11).

I have been made complete in Christ (Col. 2:10).

I have been buried, raised and made alive with Christ (Col. 2:12, 13).

I died with Christ and I have been raised up with Christ. My life is now hidden with Christ in God. Christ is now my life (Col. 3:1–4).

I have been given a spirit of power, love and self-discipline (2 Tim. 1:7).

I have been saved and set apart according to God's doing (2 Tim. 1:9; Titus 3:5).

Because I am sanctified and am one with the Sanctifier, He is not ashamed to call me brother (Heb. 2:11).

I have the right to come boldly before the throne of God to find mercy and grace in time of need (Heb. 4:16).

I have been given exceedingly great and precious promises by God by which I am a partaker of God's divine nature (2 Pet. 1:4).[4]

Isn't this cause for confidence? This is not self-help. This is God-help. This is not self-esteem, because none of these affirmations can come from self, none can be accomplished through pulling up of

---

[4] Neil T. Anderson, *Victory Over the Darkness: Realizing the Power of Your Identity in Christ* (Ventura, CA: Regal, 1990), 57–59.

bootstraps or the turning over of new leaves. These statements—and many more found in the Scriptures—are God-esteem, because they are what God does for us and what God says about us.

Jesus says something remarkable about us by virtue of something remarkable he says about himself: "I am the resurrection and the life. Whoever believes in me, though he die, yet shall he live" (John 11:25). There is no more secure position than this. If you are in Christ, you cannot be stopped even if you are killed.

Because of Christ, I am free to confess that I am a sinner deserving the wrath of God, but I am also free from both sin and wrath. Why do some Christians think that to seek our identity in Christ, the way the Scriptures say we ought to, is thinking too much of ourselves? Why are they afraid to trust what God says about them? When God says to his people, "Whoever touches you touches the apple of my eye" (Zech. 2:8), am I to think he doesn't mean it? In fact, to live in insecurity (or to insist upon it doctrinally) is to side with the accusations of the Devil, whose chief end is to convince us that our sin is greater than our God's promise to forgive it.

In Martin Luther's "Letters of Spiritual Counsel," we find this word of encouragement written to a young correspondent:

> When the devil throws our sins up to us and declares that we deserve death and hell, we ought to speak thus: "I admit that I deserve death and hell. What of it? Does this mean that I shall be sentenced to eternal damnation? By no means. For I know One who suffered and made satisfaction in my behalf. His name is Jesus Christ, the Son of God. Where he is, there shall I be also."[5]

When you see who you are through the lens of the gospel, it changes everything. But there's another dimension to gospel vision.

THE GOSPEL GIVES US A REDEMPTIVE VIEW OF PLACE

What does 1 Peter 2:9 call us? "A chosen race, a royal priesthood, a holy nation, a people for his own possession." You have perhaps

---

[5] Martin Luther, *Luther: Letters of Spiritual Counsel*, ed. and trans. Theodore G. Tappert (Vancouver, CA: Regent College, 2003), 86–87.

already noticed these are not singular nouns. (It might have been bugging you the whole time we were discussing the secure view of self.) You are right. While Peter's descriptions of our identity in this passage do tell us who we are individually in Christ, the direct thrust of the passage is not on individual status but on our *corporate* status.

We are chosen, made royal, made holy, and owned, but we are made and done so as a race, a priesthood, a nation, a people. And here we are reminded that while God saves us as individuals, he does not mean to save us to an individualistic faith. We are saved within the context of his covenant with his people; and we are saved *for* something.

Race and *nation* and *people* denote real-world implications and ramifications. Races and nations correspond to categories of creation. When God set his predestining purposes on Israel, he did so to mark them out as holy, not simply from the world but within the world. He poured his grace upon this race and nation, not just to set them apart *from* something but to set them apart *for* something, namely to be a light unto the other nations in testifying to the gospel of the glory of God. Similarly, as God grafts the Gentiles into his election of "his people," making one new man out of the two (Eph. 2:11–19), he does so as a witness to the world that God has a plan to restore it through the words and works of Jesus Christ.

It is for this reason that we are a royal priesthood. We aren't given the elevated status of having been clothed in the righteousness of Christ to lord our state over others; that would in fact imply we have merited this royal treatment, that it is our righteousness, not the foreign righteousness of the King. No, instead our royalty is a conferring of ambassadorship. As citizens of heaven now, we do the commissioned work of a "priesthood," acting as go-betweens for God to the lost nations. We have been reconciled to become ministers of reconciliation, to be witnesses to the world, to be seekers of the kingdom (which is "coming," not going), and doers of God's will (which will be done on earth as it is in heaven).

God has a special plan in Christ's atoning work on the cross and out of the tomb for the very land we inhabit. We see it first in his creation of a good earth. We see it after the fall in his commands to the Israelites regarding livestock and cultivation. We see it in the prophets as they forecast the day of Mt. Zion's glory over the nations of the world. We see it when Jesus feeds the five thousand with bread and fish, when he walks on water, when he uses mud to heal blindness, and when he calms the storm. We see it in the breaking of the earth and the reactions of the heavens when Jesus is killed. And we see it in the fallen creation's groaning for its own redemption (Rom. 8:22). But it is groaning in childbirth, Paul says—meaning, the pangs of its desperation are giving way to new life.

Jesus prays that God's kingdom would come, that his will would be done on earth as it is in heaven (Matt. 6:10). Jesus himself is in essence the answer to his prayer, for the Father has sent him to do God's will, to announce the kingdom of heaven's "at hand"-ness, and to usher in this kingdom (which is the manifest presence of God's reign) through the ministry of his sinless life, sacrificial death, and glorified resurrection. What Jesus showcases in this ministry is that through himself God is making good on his promises to Israel about the world, which is to say, about *this world*, about "the land." N. T. Wright is helpful here:

> The Land was, of course, not only a symbol: it was the source of bread and wine, the place to graze sheep and goats, grow olives and figs. It was the place where, and the means through which, YHWH gave to his covenant people the blessings he had promised them, which were all summed up in the many-sided and evocative word *shalom*, peace. It was the new Eden, the garden of YHWH, the home of the true humanity. . . . Although, as we shall see, "the kingdom of god" had as its primary referent the *fact* of YHWH's becoming King, this social context meant that the idea of divine kingship also carried the notion of the Land as the *place where* YHWH would be ruler. He would cleanse his holy Land, making it fit again for his people to inhabit, ruling the nations from it.[6]

---

[6] N. T. Wright, *The New Testament and the People of God* (Minneapolis: Fortress, 1992), 226–27.

This is what Peter is getting at by declaring our identity in the gospel as a chosen race, a royal priesthood, a holy nation, and a people for God's possession. We are restored by the gospel to our undeserving place under Christ's rightful rule of the entire cosmos. And it is why Paul includes in those who will bow to Christ's kingship every knee "in heaven and on earth and under the earth" (Phil. 2:10). If God's plan for the consummation of history is not the evacuation of Christians to disembodied bliss in a celestial paradise but is in fact the establishing of Christians as princes and princesses under the exalted reign of the radiant King in the new heavens and the new earth, we ought not to look at this world as if it is going to hell in a handbasket. God's plan is not to crumble it up and toss it in the trash bin. His plan is to straighten out its rough patches, raze its high places, and raise its low. If his plan is that the earth be covered with the knowledge of his glory like the waters cover the sea (Hab. 2:14), this means we need a glory-drenched vision of the places around us. I love the prophecy of Haggai 2:6–7:

> For thus says the LORD of hosts: Yet once more, in a little while, I will shake the heavens and the earth and the sea and the dry land. And I will shake all nations, so that the treasures of all nations shall come in, and I will fill this house with glory, says the LORD of hosts.

This is especially important for those of us living in America's New England. Once the shining jewel of Western Christendom, the land of joyous Puritanism and nose-to-the-grindstone Protestantism, New England is now the least churched, least religious part of the United States. The land of the Great Awakening is now very much asleep. The place once bathed in springs of Christ-exalting preaching is now very, very dry.

I live in Vermont, the state considered the most dry of the dry New England states, about fifteen minutes from a town called Rutland. The town's name is the town's general sense of self—a rut land. Young people here especially feel trapped, isolated, like they're in a dead end.

But if God's saving purposes in the gospel are for races, nations, peoples, and therefore lands, we know there is no such thing as a dead-end place. Indeed, since revival presupposes deadness and dryness, New England may be the most *ripe* place for God's stirring in America!

God owns all places, let's not forget. "There is not a square inch in the whole domain of our human existence," Abraham Kuyper reminds us, "over which Christ, who is Sovereign over *all*, does not cry: 'Mine!'"[7]

It is easy to lose heart among the ruins of any place, but there's a heritage here, a history, even if to see it we must go all the way back before the fall to when God said this place was "good." The gospel would have us keep that in mind, but it would also have us look forward to the day when God proves that he wins out through Christ's atoning work, that what he declared good will be remade—*sans* sickness, suffering, and societal breakdown—so that it is a land befitting its Sovereign.

The gospel gives us a realistic vision of what the world has become, but it also gives us an optimistic vision of what it will one day be. As a chosen race, a royal priesthood, a holy nation, and a people for his own possession, we are given a redemptive view of place. Perhaps like C. S. Lewis and Charles Williams, this may lead us to seeing the gospel springs beneath the rocky soil of the fallen world. Lewis and Williams favored a concept called *Logres*, which for them corresponded to the true England beneath the apparent England, the England of Arthur and Camelot and virtuous knights and questing under the banner of God and king.[8] David Downing writes:

> Lewis imagines that the title has been passed down secretly from generation to generation and that it now rests upon the one appointed to lead the battle against a new type of invasion. . . . In his Arthurian books, Williams used Logres to represent the spiritual side of England, the combination of Christian and Celtic

---

[7] Abraham Kuyper, inaugural lecture at the Free University of Amsterdam, October 20, 1880, in *Lectures on Calvinism* (Peabody, MA: Hendrickson, 2008), viii.
[8] The word *Logres* comes from the Welsh word for "England."

ideals, a force that stands against the tides of worldiness and corruption.[9]

Lewis brought this concept into his fantasy work in other ways, as well, positioning secret portals between this world and another one in now-iconic wardrobes, paintings, and train stations. The gist of the *Logres* idea is that God's original plan for the races, nations, and peoples—and the lands they inhabit—is still here, mostly obscured and hidden, but occasionally bubbling up to the surface, with the promise of one day subsuming the ruins with their truer selves. In these literary works, characters captured by a better vision—the vision of *Logres*—operate according to the true England, the truer and better sense of their place. Likewise, when we are captured by the gospel's vision, we operate according to the kingdom of heaven, which is the truer and better place, and while it is not fully here yet, it is nevertheless "at hand." Jesus tells us the kingdom of heaven will grow from little seeds into the largest plant in the garden and from a little leaven into the whole lump of dough (Matt. 13:31–33). Paul says this of the gospel: "In the whole world it is bearing fruit and increasing" (Col. 1:6).

As salt and light, then, those with the gospel's secure view of self "shall build up the ancient ruins; they shall raise up the former devastations; they shall repair the ruined cities, the devastations of many generations" (Isa. 61:4). The gospel gives us a redemptive view of place.

Neither of these visions, however, is to terminate on us or our work. The purpose of the gospel's vision of us and of our environment is a vision primarily and ultimately for the glory of God.

THE GOSPEL GIVES US AN EPIC VIEW OF GOD

First Peter 2:9 continues: "that you may proclaim the excellencies of him who called you out of darkness into his marvelous light." This is the whole point of God's saving purposes in Christ for us and our world—that we might worship God.

---

[9] David C. Downing, "That Hideous Strength: Spiritual Wickedness in High Places," in *C. S. Lewis: Life, Works, and Legacy*, vol. 2, *Fantasist, Mythmaker, and Poet*, ed. Bruce L. Edwards (Westport, CT: Praeger, 2007), 65.

The Westminster divines wanted us to know that the chief end of man is to glorify God and enjoy him forever. And Peter wants us to know that we are saved so excellently so that we will know more deeply the excellence of our Savior God. We are made much of so that we will make much of him!

But notice the wording: "excellencies," *plural*. This is because the excellencies of God are various and endless. Within each person of the Trinity there are infinite excellencies, each of which, in conjunction with the others, produces a glory the writers of the Bible simply can't shut up about. God's glory overwhelms them, consumes them, transfixes them, enthralls them, and transforms them. God's glory wrecks and undoes them. And yet still there is desire for more.

"The glory of God" becomes in the Scriptures something to proclaim, something to aim for, and something to enjoy. It is something to fear and something to take refuge in. It is big enough that the vast heavens are its proclaimer and the vast universe will be its cradle, yet is personal enough that we ought to drink and eat to commend it.

We ought to set firm in our minds that the vision the gospel gives us of ourselves and of our surroundings is only possible through the illuminating light of God. Through the gospel we see God most clearly because it is himself God wants us most to see. The redemption of people and place is meant to make us say "Whoa!"—not about people and place, but about God. Jonathan Edwards reminds us:

> If God esteems, values, and has respect to things according to their nature and proportions, he must necessarily have the greatest respect to himself. It would be against the perfection of his nature, his wisdom, holiness, and perfect rectitude, whereby he is disposed to do every thing that is fit to be done, to suppose otherwise.[10]

Throughout the Scriptures we see that God is a jealous God,

---

[10] Jonathan Edwards, *Dissertation on the End for Which God Created the World* in *The Works of President Edwards* (New York: Leavitt and Allen, 1852), 2:200.

that he is concerned for his own name's sake, that he commands our worship, that he says and does things purely as demonstrations of his own exclusive claim to godhood. We are left to surmise only that God's greatest passion is for his own glory.

How is this concern reflected in the gospel? First, the gospel of forgiveness of sins through Christ is predicated on our needing forgiveness, and further, on our inability to provide restitution to merit such pardon. So the gospel's presupposition is mankind's *lack* of glory. Sin in fact is defined as to "fall short of the glory of God" (Rom. 3:23). Second, though, Christ the God-man himself makes this restitution for us on the cross, which gives God the glory (the credit) for salvation. Third, he goes to the cross willingly; nobody murders him except that he has allowed them to, which takes the infamy of blame off of the perpetrators and transfers it to the credit of the sacrifice. Fourth, the God-man doesn't stay dead but rises on the third day through the power of the Spirit, with a glorified body. Ergo, even more glory for God. Then he ascends into heaven, giving himself even more glory. He sends the Spirit to grant us the gift of faith in receiving Christ's work, so that he would get even more glory in the gospel's acceptance. He sees that the gospel spreads into the farthest reaches of the earth, because he wants even more glory. And finally, he will return again to establish his kingdom once for all (lots of glory there), judging the quick and the dead (even more glory), and replacing the sun with the radiance of God's glory (Heb. 1:3) as the literal light of the new heavens and new earth (glory saturation approaching 100 percent). At each point in the gospel's design, implementation, application, and forecast, God is at the very center taking the credit and establishing his own centrality. Indeed, we could say that God is himself God-centered, and while the gospel is for our salvation, it is chiefly for God's own glory.

He has called us in the gospel from darkness to his marvelous light. This light is marvelous because it is something to marvel at. This marveling in gospel illumination is just the tip of the iceberg of proclaiming God's multiple excellencies. At every point of it we see how God is excellent in forethought, how he is excellent in Christ's sinless life, how he is excellent in Christ's sacrificial death, how he is excellent in Christ's resurrection, how he is excellent even in judgment of the unrepentant rejecters of the gospel. Every angle of the gospel we look at ends up showing us a different reflection of God's glory.

The gospel, then, begins and ends and brims top to bottom with the glory of God.

John Piper concludes, therefore, that "God is most glorified in us when we are most satisfied in Him."[11]

Maybe we feel small and sluggish, defeated and doubtful; maybe we feel like we're at a dead end or cul-de-sac, in a rut, in a place with no future or potential; maybe we can't see ourselves and our environment through gospel eyes because our vision of God is too small.

The truth is that we are starving for the glory of God. We wake up and are stirred when we get a glimpse of the bigness of God, and only the bigness of the gospel is designed to do that.

The gospel in fact is scaled to the very shape of God himself.

---

[11]John Piper, *The Dangerous Duty of Delight* (Sisters, OR: Multnomah, 2001), 20.

Chapter Three

THE GOD-SHAPED GOSPEL

"He therefore that will be saved, must thus think of
the Trinity."—from the Athanasian Creed

I can still remember the smell of the carpet of our guest bedroom
in our home outside Nashville, Tennessee. It was a light, fuzzy-
looped Berber with specks of gray-toned blues and reds to better
hide stains, and it held the faint but acrid mélange of carpet glue
and dust and the residual scent of burnt rubber from the vacuum
cleaner belt. You would not have noticed this smell unless you
had spent many hours with your nose buried in it as I had. But I
remember it well, and the harsh indents of its surface in my fore-
head and chin.

There is a sublime juxtaposition in the man prostrate on the
floor groaning prayers too deep for words, a joining of hard surface and gentle ether, of earth and heaven. Something big belying
a guest bedroom in a suburban neighborhood happens when a
man gets his soul naked before God, when his nose is running and
his throat is hurting and his hands are trembling and he would
be flailing if not for his grasp on a thread attached to the hem
of Christ's garment. This man—vulnerable, exposed, empty of
strength and possession and merit—can experience a sense of the
full weight of God.

And there I was. Ripe with unsuccess, brimming with shame,
overflowing with conviction, rich with desperation. The years of
sin I'd poured into my marriage and my life in general culminated
in the emptiness of that room over a series of scattered nights over
a length of months, gathering spiritual steam for one climactic
night where the word "please" covered the extent of my prayer and
my nose filled with the tangy, earthy smell of that carpet, and at

the peak of my valley, I was finally swallowed up in the presence of God in a way fresher than ever before or ever since.

I brought my nothingness to the floor beneath God's table. And he brought himself.

I did not hear it audibly, but clear as a bell the Holy Spirit of God spoke to my heart, "I love you and I approve of you."

I believed him. By his grace, I believed his grace. I knew he did not approve of my sin or my righteousness, I knew he approved of me only in the righteousness of his son Jesus, but the approval of God was the exact thing I needed to hear, know, and feel. I felt for the first time in a very long time *covered*. Safe and secured.

What was happening? I had been pushed to give my whole self to God. I had no other choice, really. None of my idols had panned out. My crutches had been mercifully kicked out from under me. The IVs had been yanked from my veins. Sin left a bitter taste in my mouth. There was not much left of me, but all I had was weakly thrust godward. And as my whole self was offered to God on the Berber altar, his whole self took me up.

C. S. Lewis reflects:

An ordinary simple Christian kneels down to say his prayers. He is trying to get into touch with God. But if he is a Christian he knows that what is prompting him to pray is also God: God, so to speak, inside him. But he also knows that all his real knowledge of God comes through Christ, the Man who was God—that Christ is standing beside him, helping him to pray, praying for him. You see what is happening. God is the thing to which he is praying—the goal he is trying to reach. God is also the thing inside him which is pushing him on—the motive power. God is also the road or bridge along which he is being pushed to that goal. So that the whole threefold life of the three-personal Being is actually going on in that ordinary little bedroom where an ordinary man is saying his prayers.[1]

Yes.

---

[1] C. S. Lewis, *Mere Christianity* (Westwood, NJ: Barbour, 1952), 139–40.

We should not be surprised to find God so readily available to us with the fullness of himself, because he has built within us a reflection of his wholeness: "Then God said, 'Let us make man in our image, after our likeness'" (Gen. 1:26). The one true God is a unity of diversity, a diversity in unity. When he says "our image" and "our likeness" he is saying "my image" and "my likeness." He is not referring to himself and the angelic host any more than he is referring to himself and other gods. "So God created man in his own image" (Gen. 1:27). Verse 26 tells us the singular God's intention to make man in *their* image, and verse 27's "so" begins the statement telling us that he followed through. That the plural pronoun is used in verse 26 and the singular in verse 27 does not mean there are multiple images. It means that the Trinity is right there, in the shadows of Genesis 1. And he is right here, in the shadows of us.

What does it mean to be made in God's image? I don't rightly know. Is it that our body, mind, and soul illustrate the tri-unity of God? Is it that we are the only creatures who can reason or who have a spiritual consciousness? Is it that we are the only creatures that create for glory's sake? Is it that man has a dominion of the earth reflective of God's dominion over all existence? The answer may be all of the above. The Bible does not tease out all the ways of the *Imago Dei*.

Because of our rebellion against God, he says to himself, "Man has become like one of us" in a different way, with an awareness of sin (Gen. 3:22). But God's knowledge of good and evil is a holy knowledge, a sovereign knowledge. He is over evil but not its author or its object. In our vulnerability to and embrace of sin, we are both victims and authors. We reflect the image of God now as if by broken glass.

None of this is to say that God is within every man in the pantheistic or pluralistic sense. When New Agers say God is in everyone, they really mean that God *is* everyone. When Christians say that everyone is made in the image of God, we mean that we were created to reflect a sense of the diversity in unity that is God himself. There is an inherent dignity and sanctity in this image for even the vilest pagan, elect or not.

When God redeems a man, then, he puts himself inside that man, but not in divinizing him. He puts himself inside that man in the sense of restoring the image of himself that sin broke and obscured. Knowing this, we can say that "salvation comes from God" means "salvation comes from the Trinity." And we can say that the restorative work of the gospel is carried out by the full measure of that Trinity.

THE SHAPE OF THE TRINITY

We ought to know what the Trinity is. There is ample help with this task. Informed by the authoritative Scriptures, the creeds and the church fathers help us understand that the orthodox view of the Trinity can be outlined like this:

- There is one God.
- There are three distinct persons who are God—the Father, the Son, and the Holy Spirit.
- Each of these persons is equally, eternally, and simultaneously God.

There is much more that can be said about the Trinity, but this is the minimum qualifying for orthodoxy. Of course we should not expect to understand how this Trinitarian reality works, but we can still acknowledge that it does. We have all the information needed to say what the Trinity is even if we can't say *how* it is. I don't understand what Connie Eaton does at her desk, nose deep in spreadsheets and the tax code, but I understand that she handles my taxes.

Each person of the Trinity is fully God, each holding the same divine *essence*, to use the catholic parlance. They dance. The Son serves to glorify the Father, deferring and submitting to his will, despite his equality with the Father. The Spirit serves to glorify the Son, seeking to glorify the Father through him, despite his equality with both Father and Son. The Father glorifies himself through the sending of the Son and the Spirit despite his equality with them. Together, the one true God glorifies himself in a community of delight and deference, each person relating and reflecting, distinguished by their roles and missions, unified by their simultaneous and equal and eternal godness. There are not three gods; there is one God existing in three persons.

The eternally begotten Son—begotten, not made—proceeds from the Father. The Spirit proceeds from the Father and the Son. (Can you *filioque* me, dawg?) While each person fulfills distinct purposes, none is subservient to or deficient from another. Calvin, paraphrasing Tertullian, notes that "there is a kind of distribution or economy in God which has no effect on the unity of essence."[2] They are not each one-third of God, nor is God tripolar. Three persons eternally exist as one God. This is orthodox Trinitarianism, and we mustn't fudge on any of the details or we will lose the real shape of the Trinity.

As I edit this chapter, popular religious spokesperson T. D. Jakes, overseer of The Potter's House in Dallas, Texas, is all over my blog subscription feed because of his invitation to a particular Christian conference. Jakes has a background in Oneness Pentecostalism, which is traditionally known for its view of the Trinity commonly classified as modalism.

Modalists maintain that there is one God and that he exists in three Persons—Father, Son, and Holy Spirit—but not simultaneously. Instead, modalists use language like "God exists in three manifestations," inferring that God is sometimes Father, sometimes Son, and sometimes Holy Spirit. This view has always been untrue, but was officially declared a heresy (twice) by the church in the fourth century. The "sometimes" of modalism's manifestation language is at odds with both Scripture and the verbiage of the creeds. Here, as an example, is a taste of the Athanasian Creed's Trinitarian confession:

> And the catholic faith is this: That we worship one God in Trinity,
> and Trinity in unity;
>   Neither confounding the persons nor dividing the substance.

---

[2] John Calvin, *Institutes of the Christian Religion*, ed. John T. McNeill, trans. Ford Lewis Battles, 2 vols. (Philadelphia: Westminster, 1960), 1:128.

For there is one person of the Father, another of the Son, and another of the Holy Spirit.

But the godhead of the Father, of the Son, and of the Holy Spirit is all one, the glory equal, the majesty coeternal.

When the Athanasian Creed speaks of the three persons of the Trinity having coeternal majesty, it denies a God who morphs into one of three persons at a time.

Now, T. D. Jakes wishes to distance himself from his Oneness Pentecostal background. He desires a wider audience. So he claims that his view has evolved from his heterodox foundations. But the language in his church's statement of faith on the Trinity still includes the fuzzy, red-flaggy "manifestations," and when Jakes attempts to differentiate himself from Oneness Pentecostalism, he nevertheless neglects to distance himself from it, finding it difficult to clearly state his personal view of the Trinity to the exclusion of his reputedly former view out of fear of hurting the feelings of those in his Oneness past.[3] In 2000, he denied in a statement to *Christianity Today* that he is a modalist, but in fifteen paragraphs he nowhere articulates simple orthodox Trinitarianism.[4] He affirms that there is one God and that Father, Son, and Holy Spirit are distinct, both of which are good affirmations, but he cannot seem to put the two together to distinguish between three-in-one and one-at-a-time. Ten years later Jakes is pressed by Open House interviewer Sheridan Voisey to stake out his perspective, but Jakes claims the Trinity is hard to define.[5] In his most recent public statements, at the Elephant Room 2 online conference, Jakes assents to Trinitarian questioning but nevertheless continues to fail to openly repudiate the Oneness heresy. In all of this, we should remember it is not difficult to confess orthodox Trinitarianism, for those who want to do it.

The shape of the Trinity is in the shadows of the Old Testament,

---

[3] "Belief Statement," The Potter's House, http://www.thepottershouse.org/Local/About-Us/Belief-Statement.aspx.

[4] T. D. Jakes, "My Views on the Godhead," *Christianity Today Online* (February 1, 2000), http://www.christianitytoday.com/ct/2000/februaryweb-only/13.0b.html.

[5] T. D. Jakes, interview by Sheridan Voisey, *Open House*, July 18, 2010, http://downloads.fm1032.com.au/oh/oh_TDJakes2010-07-18.mp3.

but we do not live in the Old Testament anymore. In the covenant of grace, we know that the plural *Elohim* is the singular God who exists eternally as Father, Son, and Holy Spirit. The Hebrews knew that the word for "one" in the Shema—"Hear, O Israel: the LORD our God, the LORD is one"—is *'ehād*, a unified collective (like the words "earth" and "water"). We know in the light of progressive revelation that what is collected in this unity is God the Father, God the Son, and God the Spirit. In Isaiah 48, one who identifies himself saying "I am the first, and I am the last" (v. 12) also says the Lord God and the Spirit have sent him (v. 16). Who can be both sent by the Lord God and his Spirit and also be the first and the last? We know that Isaiah's prophecy dawns into the Light of the World, Jesus.

There and elsewhere in the Old Testament is the Trinity, smoldering beneath the ashes of the old covenant sacrifices, his number hidden in single-file tracks in the sand, encoded in the language, enshrouded in the symbols. Now here is the Trinity, revealed in the light of the Son who comes that we might be free indeed, free to know God more fully in the fullness of his plan for the revelation of the fullness of himself. And still in the new covenant clarity we see only dimly, waiting for the time we will see more fully still.

Is this important? Should we just leave Bishop Jakes alone? No, we should implore him earnestly to come out of the shadows of obfuscation—or the absolute darkness of heresy, if that's where he is—and embrace the light of orthodox Trinitarianism.

Understanding the Trinity is important because if we want a real relationship with God we must make sure it's really God we're in a relationship with. We want to know who God is and what he's like as best as we can.

In following Jesus, we are being transformed from one degree of glory to another (2 Cor. 3:18), which is a way of saying that we are more and more reflecting what it means to be made in God's image. If we are his image bearers, we will want to know the shape of his image. God is the Trinity, so if we want to glorify God, we have to get the Trinity right.

BAPTIZED IN THE SINGULAR NAME
OF THE PLURAL DIVINE

Back to that guest bedroom. In the cleft of my rock, shielding my eyes in the abrasive cushion of the floor, the backside of God's glory came by in the proclamation of his restoring gospel. Wholeness is an aim of the gospel (1 Thess. 5:23) and completeness is an aim of God's words (2 Tim. 3:16–17), so God's wholeness and completeness are brought to bear, condescending in Trinitarian concert. It is from his fullness that "we have all received grace upon grace" (John 1:16).

When Jesus commissions his disciples to make disciples of all nations, he commands them to baptize "in the name of the Father and of the Son and of the Holy Spirit" (Matt. 28:19). It is worth mentioning that *name* is singular—it is "the name" of the Trinity, not "names."

In the Acts of the Apostles we see that converts appear to be baptized simply "in the name of Jesus." Whether any baptismal invocation—I hesitate to use the word "formula" here—was ever intended by Jesus and, if it was, whether the apostles actually shortened it as reports suggest, we may not know, but it makes sense in light of our understanding of gospel conversion to connect "in Jesus's name" to "in the name of the Father, Son, and Spirit," because Jesus is the doorway into the life of God.[6] At our church, we close many prayers "in Jesus's name, Amen" because we acknowledge that our access to communion with the Father was purchased and secured by the Son. But we also close some corporate prayers by saying "in your Son, by your Spirit, and for your glory, Amen" because we want to, as Fred Sanders says, "pray with the grain."[7]

The Son is not the Father and the Spirit, but baptizing in Jesus's name is not at odds with baptizing in the name of the Trinity, because as the way to the Father, the truth for the Father, and the

---

[6] See the discussions in D. A. Carson, *Matthew Chapters 13 through 28*, Expositor's Bible Commentary (Grand Rapids, MI: Zondervan, 1995), 597–98; and Robert H. Gundry, *Matthew: A Commentary on His Handbook for a Mixed Church under Persecution* (2nd ed., Grand Rapids, MI: Eerdmans, 1994), 596.

[7] Fred Sanders, *The Deep Things of God: How the Trinity Changes Everything* (Wheaton, IL: Crossway, 2010), 211–39.

life from the Father, and as the Spirit-anointed Messiah of God, Jesus is our doorway to the fullness of God. The Father sends the Son that we might know and be reconciled to the Father, that the Father might be glorified, but also that the Son might return to send the Spirit that we might know the Son and be reconciled through the Son to the Father, that they may be in us and we may be in them as they are in each other (John 17).

Selah.

Why baptize in the name of the Trinity? There are a few possible reasons:

First, Jesus's own baptismal scene is populated with the Trinitarian presence (Matt. 3:16–17). The Son is in the water, the Father is speaking from on high, and the Spirit descends from heaven like a dove. The fullness of deity makes its cameo at the official commissioning of Christ's proclamational ministry. Our baptism doesn't just follow the image of his death and resurrection, it follows the example of his own baptism.

Second, we baptize in the name of the Trinity because baptism is a public submission to the lordship of God, and the lordship of God involves the Trinitarian reign of the godhead. We submit not to the Father's will, the Son's leadership, and the Spirit's power as we would to items on the buffet line at Shoney's, but all together and all at once. Triune lordship is a package deal.

Third, we are baptized into the name of the Trinity because baptism marks entrance into the covenant community of the visible church, which is a picture of the covenant community of the invisible godhead.

Last, but by no means least, we are baptized in the name of the Father, the Son, and the Holy Spirit because the salvation that baptism signifies is the work of all three members of the godhead.

The gospel announces restoration of the triune image in us, which is carried out by the tri-unity of God. The content of the gospel power is designed, secured, and enacted by the Trinity. J. I. Packer connects the dots succinctly:

> God is triune: there are within the Godhead three Persons: the
> Father, the Son, and the Holy Spirit, and the work of salvation is
> one in which all three act together, the Father purposing redemp-
> tion, the Son securing it, and the Spirit applying it.[8]

There is the God-shaped gospel. There we see that salvation is
Trinitarian. The utterly depraved are utterly saved by the utterly
holy, the God who is three-times holy (Isa. 6:3; Rev. 4:8).

THE TRINITARIAN GOSPEL

There is perhaps no soul in the church more simultaneously sincere and ignorant as the one who cannot see harmony between
the theological and the practical. I pastor a church of dairy farm-
ers, carpenters, drywall installers, mechanics, and the like. When
I tell the men they ought to be the resident theologians in their
homes, you ought to see the raised eyebrows. They can see how
theology might be practical for pastors. Pastors are expected to
specialize in the impractical. But for the life of them, many men
in my neck of the woods—and yours—cannot see how the Trinity
might be as imminently helpful as the boiling of sap or connecting the electric fence to the solar panel. I am generalizing, of
course. I am grateful for all the people in my church, men and
women alike, and I'm grateful to pastor a church that finds theology important, even if they cannot always see its practicality.
Now, obviously theology is not practical in the same way as build-
ing or fixing things, but it is practical in a similar way. Theology
helps us not eternally die. John Piper says he does not aim to be
immediately practical but eternally helpful, but I would suggest
that because orthodox theology is the latter it is also undeniably
the former.[9]

The Trinitarian gospel is eternally helpful because it safeguards
us from eternal condemnation; it is immediately practical because
it does so at the moment of faith, which may be *right now*. There is
nothing more practical than the thing that keeps us alive.

---

[8]J. I. Packer, *Knowing God* (Downer's Grove, IL: InterVarsity, 1973), 15.
[9]John Piper, "God So Loved the World, Part 2" (sermon, Bethlehem Baptist Church,
Minneapolis, March 10, 2009), http://www.desiringgod.org/resource-library/sermons/
god-so-loved-the-world-part-2.

The gospel announces the fullness of God for the fullness of man despite the fullness of sin. We see Peter sharing this gospel in 1 Peter 1:1–2:

> Peter, an apostle of Jesus Christ, To those who are elect exiles of the Dispersion in Pontus, Galatia, Cappadocia, Asia, and Bithynia, according to the foreknowledge of God the Father, in the sanctification of the Spirit, for obedience to Jesus Christ and for sprinkling with his blood: May grace and peace be multiplied to you.

Can there be any more helpful news for an exile to know than that he is elect? Peter addresses the Christians in the dispersion as "elect exiles." Election is extremely practical for the exile. What is more helpful for the dispossessed to know than that he is loved, chosen, approved, and secured?

But how does an exile become elect? Peter shows us the working of redemption in the work of the triune God:

> *. . . according to the foreknowledge of God the Father.*

Of God's foreknowledge John Calvin says, "This is the fountain."[10] Foreknowledge is the wellspring from which the rest of God's saving work flows. Foreknowledge can be prescience, a divine foreknowing. God foreknows what you will have for breakfast tomorrow morning, for example, or that you will not live till breakfast, for another example. But this is not the kind of foreknowledge at play in 1 Peter 1:2. As in Romans 8:29, this is about *whom* God foreknows, not what. This is relational foreknowledge.

Wayne Grudem says we could read the first clause of 1 Peter 1:2 to say, "according to God's fatherly care before the world was made."[11] In other words, Peter is revealing to us that God's disposition toward the elect is love from eternity past. If you are a Christian, God was loving you as a Father before time began.

---

[10] John Calvin, *Commentaries on the Catholic Epistles*, trans. John Owen (New York: Cosimo, 2007), 24.
[11] Wayne Grudem, *1 Peter*, Tyndale New Testament Commentary (Grand Rapids, MI: Zondervan, 1999), 50.

Before the universe was created, he saw you at your worst and said, "I love you."

The gospel of the Father's foreknowledge is a very helpful theology because it reminds us that God did not adopt us based on our faith, but that we exercised faith based on his adoption. Paul writes in Galatians 4:6, "And *because you are sons*, God has sent the Spirit of his Son into our hearts, crying, 'Abba! Father!'" The gospel begins in the Father's love for his children as his children before they are his children. In the eternal now, the Christian is God's child, which ensures that the elect who in time are condemned objects of wrath will in time become redeemed objects of mercy (Eph. 2:1–4). Even the good works we do after conversion were devised in eternity past by God himself, "prepared beforehand" (Eph. 2:10) for our exercise in time.

If this kind of foreknowledge is true, we have tremendous cause for assurance and security. God predestines to salvation those he foreknows, and what God predestines cannot not take place; otherwise he is not God or predestination means something more like guesswork.

Christians are saved according to God's foreknowledge and also:

. . . in the sanctification of the Spirit.

The Trinity saves us by God's foreknowledge. And the Trinity saves us in the sanctification of the Holy Spirit.

The Spirit has us covered. There are two senses of the Spirit's sanctifying work, the first of which is the initial cleansing at conversion. In this sense for Christians, sanctification is past tense. Consider 1 Corinthians 6:11: "But you were washed, you were sanctified, you were justified in the name of the Lord Jesus Christ and by the Spirit of our God." But there is another aspect to the Spirit's cleansing work, what is typically referred to as "progressive sanctification." In the first sense, we are given a new nature at the new birth, the Spirit having cleansed our conscience and implanted his purifying presence within us, sealing us as God's possession and securing us for eternity. But we have in us still the sinful nature.

The sinful nature wars with our spirit, but the Holy Spirit sustains us, and through the peculiar work of comforting, convicting, and illuminating, he continues to make us holier.

First Corinthians 15:1–2 shows us the two senses: the gospel was received (past tense), is stood upon (present tense), and is saving us (present-future). We have been justified, yes; we have been sanctified, yes. But there is still this matter of "bringing holiness to completion" (2 Cor. 7:1). There is still the fruit of the Spirit to bear. The Westminster Larger Catechism's seventh question spells it out thusly:

> Sanctification is a work of God's grace, whereby they whom God has, before the foundation of the world, chosen to be holy, are in time, through the powerful operation of his Spirit applying the death and resurrection of Christ unto them, renewed in their whole man after the image of God; having the seeds of repentance unto life, and all other saving graces, put into their hearts, and those graces so stirred up, increased, and strengthened, as that they more and more die unto sin, and rise unto newness of life.

The converting work is accumulating and increasing in intensity. The Father foreknows us as his children and therefore elects us to receive the Spirit's resurrecting stir, effectual call, indwelling presence, and purifying sustenance. The Holy Spirit quickens our hearts, convicts us to repent of the sin he enables us to taste as bitter, compels us to follow the Savior he enables us to taste as delicious, and fans the flame of refining holiness. But the Spirit on behalf of the Trinity does not point to himself. He glorifies the Son:

> . . . *for obedience to Jesus Christ and for sprinkling with his blood.*

First, a gospel note: we are saved *for* obedience, not *by* it. See, again, Ephesians 2:10. Heed Augustine: "For grace is given not because we have done good works, but in order that we may have power to do them."[12]

The purpose of the Father is that the purpose of the Spirit is

---

[12] Quoted in *Ancient Christian Commentary on Scripture*, New Testament vol. 6, *Romans*, ed. Gerald Bray (Downer's Grove, IL: InterVarsity, 1998), 276.

that the purpose of the Christian is to be committed to the purposes of Christ. The Spirit proceeds from the Father and the Son in order to conform us to the image of Christ in order that God would be magnified. This magnification takes place in our obedience to Jesus, as good works glorify our Father in heaven (Matt. 5:16). And this magnification takes place in our being sprinkled with his blood, because to be made holy is to better reflect the image of God.

The Son has come from the Father in the power of the Spirit to die that men may be reconciled to the Father in the power of the Spirit. He provides the sacrifice, the Father accepts the sacrifice, and the Spirit applies the sacrifice to us. At the cross, as Jesus is nailed to the intersection of God's wrath and mercy, he feels the Father's desertion but commits his hand to the Father's Spirit nonetheless. Christ is the agent of the Trinity's dramatic scheming against man's rebellion; he is the servant of God's stratagem. He smuggles divinity into humanity that humanity, by God's grace and power, might be taken up. Francis Schaeffer writes:

> I think the cry of Jesus, "My God, my God, why hast thou forsaken me?" indicated that God in His great love was willing to allow the division which came between God and man in the Fall to be carried up into the Trinity itself and there conquered.[13]

Do you see how the Trinity hems us in? We have no defense against this brilliant triangle offense. Praise Jesus! "The salvation that was *planned* by the Father has been *procured* by the Son and is now *presented* and *protected* by the Spirit."[14]

The glory of God is exponentially and eternally magnified by God's triune self. "Holy, holy, holy, is the Lord God Almighty, who was and is and is to come!" (Rev. 4:8). His holiness is threefold-perfection deep and wide and high and long. "Holy, holy, holy is the LORD of hosts; the whole earth is full of his glory!" (Isa. 6:3). One day the knowledge of God's glory will cover the earth like the waters cover the sea (Hab. 2:14). He will have the universe

---

[13] Quoted in *Letters of Francis Schaeffer*, ed. Lane Dennis (Wheaton, IL: Crossway, 1985), 127.
[14] Philip Ryken and Michael LeFebvre, *Our Triune God* (Wheaton, IL: Crossway, 2011), 21.

covered from every angle—it's divine geometry—as he has us covered now:

May grace and peace be multiplied to you.

The Trinitarian gospel is immediately practical because it entails that Christ is our advocate (1 John 2:1) and intercessor (Heb. 7:25) at this very moment and that the Spirit also is buttressing our prayers (Rom. 8:26).

With salvation's rapture into the life of the Trinity, God isn't just commanding us to grace and peace, he is praying for it himself to himself, he is bestowing it himself through himself, he is declaring it himself through himself authoritatively. The result of salvation is that "those who are elect exiles according to God's foreknowledge, the Spirit's sanctification, and the Son's atoning work" receive grace and peace in multiplying (by threes?) abundance. This is incredibly good news.

We are saved from God to God by God through God for God. The godhead works in concert so that salvation will engulf you in God.

THE THREE-PERSONAL LIFE

John Updike crafts a meditative reflection on the simultaneous zeal and sobriety of radical Islam in his penultimate novel *Terrorist*, which tells the story of Ahmad Ashmawy Mulloy, the bastard son of an absentee Muslim father and a free-spirited Irish mother. Through the discipleship of his local imam, Ahmad finds himself compelled both inwardly and outwardly into a terrorist plot to blow up the Lincoln Tunnel in New York City. Those familiar with Updike's work know he is a brilliant merger of the religious and the earthy, the sublime and the soiled, but his subjects are typically of the Christian persuasion, Protestants to be specific, New England Protestants to be specific even more. Inspired by the events of 9/11, which Updike witnessed firsthand from the tenth floor of a Brooklyn Heights apartment, *Terrorist* trains his penetrating gaze on a working class Muslim youth, but what he finds there is a different dynamic, a different sensation, a different relationship between sinful man and holy God than what he typically finds among the adulterers, drunks, and compassionless parents in his Christ-haunted New England.

Is Ahmad's Allah near? Yes, "closer than the vein in his neck,"[15] Updike reveals at several points. He is personal but not very personable. Ahmad does believe God loves him, but he does not appear so much driven by this love as driven to achieve it. He is, mainly, pragmatic. He is working *for* his salvation with fear and trembling. Devotion is a series of hoops to jump through, the test of his worthiness.

The terrorist of the novel, then, is not Ahmad primarily but his god, who is made in the ambivalent image of the father he doesn't know. Even the companion presence of Ahmad's god is a gnawing sense of loneliness!

> In the solitude of the cab he is not alone, God is with him. But God is Himself alone, He is the ultimate of solitude. Ahmad loves his lonely God.[16]

Updike's Trinitarianism is showing. Praise God for our un-lonely God! He is eternally self-sufficient; he neither needs nor lacks. And bound up in his boundless self is the divine tri-unity of the three persons who are God. God is himself in community; he is the ultimate of relationship. Our un-lonely God loves us. And he is not just personal but personable, desiring relationship, reconciling us to himself, safeguarding and comforting us, making us friends with himself. This is all in the depths of his powerful gospel.

As I faced the great unknown of my life in that guest bedroom, eaten up by the uncertain future of my marriage, suffocated by the weight of my sin and shame, the solitude was overwhelming. I felt squashed. So there I was, face in the floor, that acrid smell lounging in my nose, hands seeking purchase in the tight looms of the carpet, as if the whole thing might give way beneath me at any moment. Even the stasis of the emptiness inside and the aloneness outside could not alleviate the pressure. I was being

---

[15] John Updike, *Terrorist* (New York: Ballantine, 2006), 152.
[16] Ibid., 211.

afflicted. But not crushed. The love of the Father was mine. The fountain of his foreknowledge, flowing from eternity past, poured into that room, pouring over me. Christ the King, my brother and my friend, my Savior and my Lord, put the warming cloak of his righteousness over my body, covering my shame, that the sweet guarantor, the Holy Spirit, might proclaim to the depths of my heart, "I approve of you."

My external circumstances did not change. But the resulting rapture of that moment was unlike anything I've ever experienced. Our big God made friends with me.

The companionship of our God is cause for great exultation. He welcomes us into God-shaped community through the God-shaped gospel.

Lewis will have the first word in the next chapter, and we will let him have the last word here:

> You may ask, "If we cannot imagine a three-personal Being, what is the good of talking about Him?" Well, there isn't any good talking about Him. The thing that matters is being actually drawn into that three-personal life, and that may begin any time—tonight, if you like.[17]

---

[17] C. S. Lewis, *Mere Christianity* (Westwood, NJ: Barbour, 1952), 139.

Chapter Four

AT PLAY IN THE FIELDS OF THE LORD

"In commanding us to glorify Him,
God is inviting us to enjoy Him."—C. S. Lewis[1]

When Pastor Matt Chandler shares online what text he will be preaching from next at The Village Church, he will sometimes then invite people to attend the worship service by saying, "Come play." I like that a lot. If it is true that when God's people gather to exalt him together, he is in the midst of them in a special way, then great joy waits for us in doing so, for, "At thy right hand there are pleasures for evermore" (Ps. 16:11 KJV).

It is not out of bounds to think of hearing the gospel proclaimed as *playing* if we are receiving the word with gladness, savoring its declarations like honey, joyfully submitting to its authority, and reveling in the infinite excellencies of its Author. Authentic worship is in many ways a childlike wonder. When we are fixated on the greatness of God, we become caught up, un-self-conscious, utterly and joyfully dependent, without pretense or worry. From N. T. Wright:

> Worship is humble and glad; worship forgets itself in remembering God; worship celebrates the truth as God's truth, not its own. True worship doesn't put on a show or make a fuss; true worship isn't forced, isn't half-hearted, doesn't keep looking at its watch, doesn't worry what the person in the next pew may be doing. True worship is open to God, adoring God, waiting for God, trusting God even in the dark.[2]

[1]C. S. Lewis, *Reflections on the Psalms* (San Diego: Harcourt Brace, 1986), 97.
[2]N. T. Wright, *For All God's Worth: True Worship and the Calling of the Church* (Grand Rapids, MI: Eerdmans, 1997), 9.

Wright's scope for worship extends beyond the scheduled corporate gathering of the church, of course, as does the Bible's scope for worship. If one day the earth will be covered with the knowledge of God's glory as the waters cover the sea (Hab. 2:14), worship is for every nook and cranny of human existence.

The cumulative effect of the gospel is affectionate worship of the one true God. The grand design of gospel proclamation, then, is gospel enthrallment, gospel enjoyment.

The best preaching exults in the Scriptures so that hearers will know that worship is the only proper response to who God is and what he's done. Preachers are laboring for the joy of the hearer, after all (2 Cor. 1:24). Exultational preaching is an act of worship itself, the proclaimer faithfully expositing the Bible while enjoying it at the same time, speaking its God-breathed words as if they were delicious, reflecting on them and reacting to them as if no words were ever more impressive, staggering, powerful. Because none are.

The best worship, then, exults in who God is and what he's done both in the corporate exaltation of a church service and in the private devotion at the foot of the bed in the dark of night or at the breakfast table in the coffee-poured ripeness of dawn. The best worship exults in who God is and what he's done in hour four of data entry in the gray cubicle as well as in the timeless revelry of the sun-dappled field or by the glittering mountain stream. The best worship exults in who God is and what he's done in the sharing of the gospel with the lost, in works of justice, works of service, or no works at all. Because the joy of the Lord is our strength.

As disciples spread out over the inhabited world, planting churches in the American rust belt, planting the gospel in the dangerous recesses of the Amazon, planting the seeds of their blood in Mohammedan deserts far afield, as they love and serve and teach and pray and die, they are beckoning, "Christ is risen! His kingdom's afoot! Come play!"

AND AGAIN I SAY REJOICE
If Christ is true, then boredom is a sin.

Boredom is a sin so long as Christ is infinitely beautiful. Even the angels, for whom the gospel is that strange mystery purposed not for themselves, long to look into the deep, fascinating well of its revelation (1 Pet. 1:12). Because the good news proclaims the unsearchable riches of Christ, who opens the window looking out on the eternal mystery of the Trinity, it is endlessly absorbing, dazzlingly multifaceted. When we are bored, it can be only because we have stopped looking at Jesus. He can't be boring. If we find him boring, it's because we are boring. The deficiency is ours, not his.

Boredom and his twin brother Laziness are fundamentally theological failures, which is to say they are failures of belief, of worship. Thomas Aquinas wisely says, "Sloth is a kind of sadness."[3] He has lifted the hood of the lazybones to peer at what's beneath. "There's your problem right there," he says, pointing. A worshipless heart. A joyless heart. The diagnosis is the same for the bored as for the lazy: a kind of sadness. And the prescription is the same for the bored as for the lazy: rejoice in the Lord.

Laziness is not rest; this is why there is no joy in it. But when Jesus sets us free, he really sets us free—free to work, free to love, free to rest—with happiness and delight, awe and wonder, fulfillment and satisfaction.

"The soul has a palate and a throat, else Jesus would not bid us drink," John Piper says.[4] It is not just our bodies that are built for enjoyment, but our spiritual senses, the insidest of our insides, and the problem of course is that we are bent to think our insides will have joy when our outsides do. But it doesn't work that way. It is the other way around. Food and drink will not truly satisfy our bodies until the bread and wine of Jesus's body satisfy our souls. We have incredible difficulty getting this through our thick skulls.

This is why God orders us in his Word to rejoice. Joy is an implication of the gospel, but it is not *implied* for the Christian life—it is commanded. It is not optional. A sampling of examples is revealing:

---

[3] Thomas Aquinas, *The "Summa Theologica" of St. Thomas Aquinas*, part 1, trans. Fathers of the English Dominican Province (London: R. & T. Washbourne, 1912), 432.
[4] John Piper, Twitter post, February 18, 2011, http://twitter.com/#!/JohnPiper/status/38822372786053120.

And you shall take on the first day the fruit of splendid trees, branches of palm trees and boughs of leafy trees and willows of the brook, and you shall rejoice before the LORD your God seven days. (Lev. 23:40)

And you shall sacrifice peace offerings and shall eat there, and you shall rejoice before the LORD your God. (Deut. 27:7)

Glory in his holy name; let the hearts of those who seek the LORD rejoice! (1 Chron. 16:10)

But let all who take refuge in you rejoice. (Ps. 5:11)

Be glad in the LORD, and rejoice, O righteous, and shout for joy, all you upright in heart! (Ps. 32:11)

Rejoice in the LORD, O you righteous, and give thanks to his holy name! (Ps. 97:12)

This is the day that the LORD has made; let us rejoice and be glad in it. (Ps. 118:24)

An evil man is ensnared in his transgression, but a righteous man sings and rejoices. (Prov. 29:6)

So if a person lives many years, let him rejoice in them all. (Eccles. 11:8)

It will be said on that day, "Behold, this is our God; we have waited for him, that he might save us. This is the LORD; we have waited for him; let us be glad and rejoice in his salvation." (Isa. 25:9)

But be glad and rejoice forever in that which I create. (Isa. 65:18)

Fear not, O land; be glad and rejoice, for the LORD has done great things! (Joel 2:21)

Though the fig tree should not blossom, nor fruit be on the vines, the produce of the olive fail and the fields yield no food, the flock be cut off from the fold and there be no herd in the stalls, yet I will rejoice in the LORD; I will take joy in the God of my salvation. (Hab. 3:17–18)

Shout, O Israel! Rejoice and exult with all your heart. (Zeph. 3:14)

Rejoice greatly, O daughter of Zion! (Zech. 9:9)

Rejoice and be glad, for your reward is great in heaven. (Matt. 5:12)

Rejoice that your names are written in heaven. (Luke 10:20)

Through him we have also obtained access by faith into this grace in which we stand, and we rejoice in hope of the glory of God. (Rom. 5:2)

Rejoice in hope, be patient in tribulation, be constant in prayer. (Rom. 12:12)

Rejoice with those who rejoice. (Rom. 12:15)

Likewise you also should be glad and rejoice with me. (Phil. 2:18)

Rejoice in the Lord always; again I will say, rejoice. (Phil. 4:4)

Rejoice always. (1 Thess. 5:16)

But rejoice insofar as you share Christ's sufferings. (1 Pet. 4:13)

Let us rejoice and exult and give him the glory, for the marriage of the Lamb has come, and his Bride has made herself ready. (Rev. 19:7)

Finally, brothers, rejoice. (2 Cor. 13:11)

Getting the picture?

Joy is deeper than happiness, but like happiness, joy is always circumstantial. Because the gospel is true, then, even when we aren't happy we can know the deeper joy because of the circumstances of God's goodness and love. On the permanent condition of God's unrelenting grace, joy is a permanent possibility.

So God commands it. He knows it is difficult for us to get to it, though. We have to strive to enter rest (Heb. 4:11). We must fight for joy. We must, to paraphrase Luther, beat it into our heads continually.

Indeed, *not* to rejoice is a sin. Lewis sallies forth: "I think we all sin by needlessly disobeying the apostolic injunction to 'rejoice' as much as by anything else."[5] Yes, and in fact, every other disobedience is a disobedience to the command to rejoice in the Lord. See Philippians 4:4. Rejoice in the Lord *always*, and I will say it to you a second time: Rejoice.

Thankfully, whatever God demands from his children he also supplies to his children in the gospel. There is no command to rejoice without its being joined with great cause for rejoicing.

Joy is part of the gospel deeps because it is something the gospel announces—"good news of great joy that will be for all the people" (Luke 2:10)—and it is something the gospel supplies— "These things I have spoken to you, that my joy may be in you, and that your joy may be full" (John 15:11). Joy is part of the implantation of the gospel's package deal. The Spirit takes up residence in the regenerated heart, and one of his chief products is the fruit called joy (Gal. 5:22).

The joy God puts in us and then draws forth in our life-encompassing adoration of him is full and ever-refilling. Peter describes it as "joy that is inexpressible and filled with glory" (1 Pet. 1:8), which is to say that it is too big to adequately capture with words; it is dumbstriking and soul-awing. We throw adjectives at this joy but it can't be covered; we find most of them tacky bumper-sticker clichés when put up next to it. This joy is filled with glory, pregnant with the refunding of God's attributes, brimming with some gospel-dispensed measure of the sum of his perfections, which to dispense is never to deplete. Eugene Peterson reminds us that "wonder can't be packaged, and it can't be worked up. It requires some sense of being there and some sense of engagement."[6] We don't see Christ, 1 Peter 1:8 says, but we

[5] C. S. Lewis, *The Problem of Pain* (New York: Macmillan, 1962), 67.
[6] Eugene Peterson, *Living the Resurrection: The Risen Christ in Everyday Life* (Colorado Springs: NavPress, 2006), 20.

love him and believe him anyway, a Spiritual engagement opening up the floodgates of unconquerable joy.

GOSPEL ENJOYMENT

The joy of the Lord is life-sized. It stretches from head to foot and to everything we put our hands on or minds to. The Westminster divines remind us: "The chief end of man is to glorify God and enjoy him forever." Jerry Bridges points out, "They did not say these are mankind's chief *ends*, but our chief *end*. The word is singular. Both glorifying God and enjoying Him together form one aim."[7] Were we to apply this to the authority of Paul's admonition in 1 Corinthians 10:31—"So, whether you eat or drink, or whatever you do, do all to the glory of God"—we would see how enjoying God's good gifts is a way to enjoy God himself.[8] The gospel frees us to enjoy God, but also to enjoy him in the enjoyment of his gifts. We can see this conjoining in Nehemiah.

First, some backstory. Sometime in the late sixth century or early fifth century BC, the Babylonians attacked Jerusalem and destroyed the holy city, leaving the temple, city walls, and everything else in ruins. After seven decades of captivity, many Jews returned from dispersion to repopulate the holy city. The book of Ezra reports on the rebuilding of the temple. But one hundred years after the devastation, when Nehemiah surveys the decimated fortification and learns the cause, he weeps. Hard. He sits down in the midst of the rubble and cries his guts out "for days" (Neh. 1:4).

Consider that Nehemiah has heard the news of Jerusalem's fallen walls a century after the fact. That's a serious sorrow. Imagine what kind of joy we could bring to our cities if we were moved by that kind of sorrow over their brokenness. After fasting and praying, Nehemiah leads the returned exiles in the rebuilding of the city walls. The work took fifty-two days, some of it conducted while the workmen fought off enemy attacks. It was a massive undertaking, but God's people under Nehemiah's direction worked faithfully, diligently, and wholeheartedly.

---

[7] Jerry Bridges, *The Joy of Fearing God* (Colorado Springs: Waterbrook, 1997), 253.
[8] I have much more to say about that idea in the chapter on freedom from hyperspirituality in Jared C. Wilson, *Gospel Wakefulness* (Wheaton, IL: Crossway, 2011).

When the entire work was done, all the people gathered into the square. And they asked Ezra to preach them a sermon. Not just any sermon. They asked him to preach the Pentateuch. And Ezra didn't just read it; he exposited it.

> They read from the book, from the Law of God, clearly, and *they gave the sense*, so that the people understood the reading. (Neh. 8:8)

Then the law did what the law does—softens hearts ready to receive God's word. The people were devastated. "For all the people wept as they heard the words of the Law" (Neh. 8:9).

What Nehemiah and Ezra say next is remarkable. Picking up again with the start of verse 9:

> And Nehemiah, who was the governor, and Ezra the priest and scribe, and the Levites who taught the people said to all the people, "This day is holy to the LORD your God; do not mourn or weep." For all the people wept as they heard the words of the Law. Then he said to them, "Go your way. Eat the fat and drink sweet wine and send portions to anyone who has nothing ready, for this day is holy to our Lord. And do not be grieved, for the joy of the LORD is your strength." So the Levites calmed all the people, saying, "Be quiet, for this day is holy; do not be grieved." And all the people went their way to eat and drink and to send portions and to make great rejoicing, because they had understood the words that were declared to them. (Neh. 8:9–12)

This passage encapsulates the formula for gospel enjoyment. In these four verses is the groundwork for eating and drinking to the glory of God. Because when our greatest sorrow is our own sin, our greatest happiness will be the gospel of God making us holy.

There is a very real sense in which Christians are always both sad and happy: "as sorrowful, yet always rejoicing; as poor, yet making many rich; as having nothing, yet possessing everything" (2 Cor. 6:10). In fact, focused in the right directions, godly sorrow will produce godly joy, and vice versa. Contemplating the grossness of our sin helps us to find Christ beautiful, and finding Christ beautiful helps us to contemplate our sin as gross. When the Bible commands joy, it does not mean to rule out deep repentance; it means to entail it. A heart broken over the law's conviction is a good thing, and *it's the first thing.*

You will not get to gospel enjoyment without personal brokenness. Thomas Watson says, "Christ is never sweet till sin is felt to be bitter."[9]

While a broken heart is a good thing and the first thing, however, a rejoicing heart over the gospel's freedom is a better thing. Some people apparently think that being holy ought to look like you stepped in dog doo. But if holiness makes you a sourpuss, you're doing it wrong.

> Then he said to them, "Go your way. Eat the fat and drink sweet wine and send portions to anyone who has nothing ready, for this day is holy to our Lord." (Neh. 8:10a)

Hold up. Eat fat? Drink wine? Because the day is holy?

Let's be clear that this is, of course, not an advocation of gluttony or drunkenness, but let's be honest that this is an admonition to real indulgence and enjoyment. Because the work of God is that celebratory. "Somebody lacks steak and wine? Give some to him! Don't you see what God has done?"

Surely one of the increasing benefits of progressive sanctification is the accumulation of sinless joys. If the gospel is true and we believe it, we ought to be overflowing with enjoyment of life. As Russell Moore writes, "Eat, drink, and be merry, for yesterday you were dead."[10]

> And do not be grieved, for the joy of the Lord is your strength. (Neh. 8:10b)

This isn't some trite "don't worry, be happy" jingle or "get an attitude adjustment" platitude. This is not joy in temporal circumstances. This is the Lord's joy.

Is it possible to be joyous in difficult times? The Bible assumes so:

---

[9] Thomas Watson, *Puritan Gems*, ed. John Adey (London: J. Snow and Ward, 1850), 15.
[10] Russell Moore, *Tempted and Tried: Temptation and the Triumph of Christ* (Wheaton, IL: Crossway, 2011), 75.

> In all our affliction, I am overflowing with joy. (2 Cor. 7:4)

> You joyfully accepted the plundering of your property, since you knew that you yourselves had a better possession and an abiding one. (Heb. 10:34)

> Count it all joy, my brothers, when you meet trials of various kinds. (James 1:2)

When we are truly enthralled by what God has done for us, we do not put as much stock in earthly circumstances. Take my stuff? Sure, okay. Take my health? Sure, okay. I am well pleased with the Lord. Joy in him keeps me going. "The hope of the righteous brings joy" (Prov. 10:28).

> So the Levites calmed all the people, saying, "Be quiet, for this day is holy; do not be grieved." And all the people went their way to eat and drink and to send portions and to make great rejoicing. (Neh. 8:11)

They heard the gospel and they partied. They glorified God in their eating and drinking and rejoicing.

Now, look, this is the Feast of Booths, not your baby cousin's quinceañera, but the implications are clear: God out of his holiness commands feasts. He loves them so much he makes up all kinds of them in the Old Testament for the children of Israel to obey him in observance. God mandates a good time. Not sinfully, but happily. Because God made good things and gives good things, he expects us to enjoy good things.

We are suspicious of pleasure and fun, when we ought to be suspicious of our hearts and flesh. But God is not against pleasure. He invented it. He invented it for his own glory. Because our God reigns and our Savior is King and we're going to live forever, chocolate tastes better.

The gospel rebuilds the broken ruins, providing the God-designed boundary for the God-ordained proclamation to inhabit and fill with God-sanctioned joy. The gospel story creates, which is to say *re-creates*, the prelapsarian garden of Edenic pleasure, and thus Edenic joy. The story of redemptive joy God tells in Nehemiah is just a snapshot of the grand narrative of redemptive joy God is telling in the whole of the Bible's gospel. Matthew Lee Anderson writes:

> This is a story that affirms the world in all its goodness and glory. It is a story of the excellence of creation, the theater of God's glory, and the dignity of those who bear the image of the Maker of this world. The good news frees us from the monstrous burden of conforming to an impossible beauty, while enabling us to clothe ourselves in the joy and love that makes us shine brighter than the stars in the heavens.[11]

When the Prodigal Son sits in the pigsty, in his repentance he envisions putting on the workman's coveralls for his dad's company (Luke 15:17–19). But when he returns, he receives the best robe and the fattened calf. The gospel vanquishes the law's curse. If we have put on Christ and his righteousness, we have changed out of our work clothes and put on the play clothes.

> Because they had understood the words that were declared to them. (Neh. 8:12b)

This kind of enjoyment does not come except by understanding and believing the gospel. Do you want this kind of joy? Then have the eagerness of Nehemiah's people to hear the Word, have the conviction of Nehemiah's people about your own sin, have the submission of Nehemiah's people to preaching and teaching and the gathering of worship, and have the heart to understand the infinite goodness of Jesus in the gospel.

Sometimes when I hear the gospel proudly proclaimed from a voice of utter conviction and exultation, I find the preaching so delicious, so exhilarating, I feel as though my heart will burst with joy. I did not get this heart through my own effort. Make way for Thomas Chalmers:

---

[11] Matthew Lee Anderson, *Earthen Vessels: Why Our Bodies Matter to Our Faith* (Bloomington, MN: Bethany, 2011), 230.

> We have already affirmed how impossible it were for the heart, by any innate elasticity of its own, to cast the world away from it, and thus reduce itself to a wilderness. The heart is not so constituted, and the only way to dispossess it of an old affection, is by the expulsive power of a new one.[12]

God gave me this heart in his great mercy, with his great power, through his great Spirit. He graciously reduced me to a wilderness, then flooded my soul all at once, "like streams in the Negeb!" (Ps. 126:4). Now to hear the law is to be sorrowed and to hear the gospel is to be astonished.

THE GOSPEL AND IT-NESS

Again, the first step to real gospel joy is real gospel brokenness. We cannot get to real happiness in God until we get to real despair of our sin. But once we have despaired of all sin and the gods at their genesis, we are free. Really, truly free. Free to eat fat, juicy steaks and drink rich, red wine.

In fact, we cannot really enjoy the good gifts God gives us until he as their Giver is our greatest joy. Until he as their Giver is our greatest joy, we will be left trying to enjoy his gifts for things they are not, rather than for things they are.

In *Surprised by Joy*, C. S. Lewis credited a close friend with cultivating in him "a serious, yet gleeful, determination to rub one's nose in the very quiddity of each thing, to rejoice in its being (so magnificently) what it was."[13] John Piper echoes this enjoyment of quiddity, commenting on this kind of awareness: "To wake up in the morning and be aware of the firmness of the mattress, the warmth of the sun's rays, the sound of the clock ticking, the sheer being of things . . ."[14]

If I don't believe the gospel, I will miss out on the joy of the it-ness of things. I will be looking to these things as drugs, as appetite-fillers, as fulfillers, as powers, as gods, as worshipers of the god of myself.

---

[12] Thomas Chalmers, "The Expulsive Power of a New Affection" in *The Works of Thomas Chalmers* (Philadelphia: Towar, J. and D. M. Hogan and Hogan, 1830), 384.
[13] C. S. Lewis, *Surprised by Joy* (Orlando, FL: Harcourt Brace, 1955), 193.
[14] John Piper, *Don't Waste Your Life* (Wheaton, IL: Crossway, 2003), 19.

If steak or wine or coffee or chocolate or anything else other than God is the highlight of my day or the ultimate joy of my heart, my joy is temporary, hollow, thin. But if I believe in the gospel, I can finally enjoy the chocolate-ness of chocolate and the coffee-ness of coffee. Only the gospel frees me to enjoy things as they truly now are and *as they someday will be.*

The gospel is itself a feast, the culmination of all the legal feasts and the saving sustenance behind the symbolic meal of the Lord's body at the Communion table. We have to eat his flesh and drink his blood to live, the same way we have to eat food and drink water to live. Without him we will die. But with him we are not set at the table of the divine fellowship to sip on the thin gruel of religion. We are adorned with the best robe, welcomed with a hearty slap on the back, commanded and urged and freed to feast on God's goodness.

The heart of God is vast, his grace is free, his gospel is exhilarating. Uncross your arms and unpurse your lips.

THE FELICITY OF CHRIST

John Flavel writes:

> Christ [is] the very essence of all delights and pleasures, the very soul and substance of them. As all the rivers are gathered into the ocean, which is the congregation or meeting-place of all the waters in the world: so Christ is that ocean in which all true delights and pleasures meet. . . . His excellencies are pure and unmixed; he is a sea of sweetness without one drop of gall.[15]

The two eldest Bennet sisters in Jane Austen's *Pride and Prejudice* are best friends, but their personalities are like night and day. Elizabeth is cynical, contemplative. Jane is ever optimistic, perhaps even naive. She can think of nothing bad to say about anyone. If anyone ever wrongs her, she instinctively forgives (if she can even see the wrong to begin with). In one scene, Jane and Elizabeth are celebrating Jane's engagement to be married. This exchange grabs me:

---

[15]John Flavel, *The Whole Works of the Rev. Mr. John Flavel* (London: Baynes and Son, 1820), 2:215.

"I am certainly the most fortunate creature that ever existed!" cried Jane. "Oh! Lizzy, why am I thus singled from my family, and blessed above them all! If I could but see you as happy! If there were but such another man for you!"

[Elizabeth replied:] "If you were to give me forty such men, I never could be so happy as you. Till I have your disposition, your goodness, I never can have your happiness."[16]

There is Spiritual truth here! Had we forty shiny idols to buoy our affections, still these affections could not be mustered to enduring happiness. Had we forty ways into religious devotion to God, if none of those forty were Christlikeness through gospel power, we "never could be so happy."

"Have this mind among yourselves," Paul tells us in Philippians 2:5, speaking of Christ's attitude. Weymouth renders the verse, "Let the same disposition be in you which was in Christ Jesus."

There is good news. Romans 8:29 tells us that Christians are predestined to be conformed to the image of Jesus. We *will* have his disposition.

The felicity of Christ is conferred to his bride. Through the power of his Spirit, we receive the mind of Christ and the Spirit's fruit, which may be another way to say Christ's disposition. Even the persecuted church has cause for great joy, for unbounded happiness of soul. Because they know Christ in his suffering, they know Christ in the joy set before him. They know Christ in his gospel, which is the antidote for universal despair.

Until we have his disposition, his goodness, we can never have his happiness.

This Jesus, for the joy set before him, endured even the cross (Heb. 12:2). Joy and the cross? What a provocative mystery! And to that mystery we now turn.

---

[16] Jane Austen, *Pride and Prejudice* (New York: Readers' League, n.d.), 330.

Chapter Five

THE SHARP EDGE OF
THE ATONEMENT

"D'ye know what Calvary was? what? what? what? . . .
It was *damnation*; and he took it *lovingly*."
—John Duncan[1]

It is the most shocking of narratives, and one of the most well known among holy and heathen alike. Tucked into the tumultuous topography of the Torah, the story radiates angst and awe, confusion and terror. It is a story about how worship emerges from the collision of faith and works.

The man and his only begotten son make a lonely trek up a mountainside (Genesis 22). They have entered the mountainous region of Moriah. The father sights a suitable spot a ways off; he trusts his attempts at delaying the task will be forgiven. Leaving their servants behind, the boy bears the wood for a sacrifice on his back alone. The man takes fire. And a knife.

There is a lump in the father's throat, a knot in his stomach. He is shaking. He doesn't understand, but he trusts. The boy is confused, but he submits.

Dad begins gathering stones to build an altar. He plods, not because he wants to disobey but because he feels weak. Stone by stone the monument comes together, and he lays the wood upon it.

"Dad," says the son, "I see fire and wood, but I don't see a lamb."

"God will provide," he says to the boy. And to himself.

I am imagining details, feelings. But I am not comfortable inventing what lies between the lines of Abraham's arranging of the altar and the binding of his son. The Word simply says that he

---

[1] Quoted in J. I. Packer, "The Logic of Penal Substitution" (Tyndale Biblical Theology Lecture, Tyndale House, Cambridge, UK, July 17, 1973), http://www.the-highway.com/cross_Packer.html.

"bound Isaac his son and laid him on the altar" (Gen. 22:9). Was there a struggle? Did Isaac protest? Or did he comply, meek and faithful to the prospective end?

I suspect he trusted, which is so unreasonable it hurts my heart and thrills it at the same time. We are standing in the light now, the radiance of God's glory shining back to that inconceivable moment, and we see in the fulfillment that the only begotten son goes willingly to be sacrificed, like a lamb to the slaughter. Perhaps even Isaac could not understand his own compliance. His "truer and better" did not attend to the cross without anguish and anxiety, so he knows and we know that obedience of will does not preclude distress of heart.

In any event, there he is on the altar. There is his father's knife overhead.

And there is the voice of "the angel of the LORD," perhaps the Son of God himself, breaking through the heavens like lightning, saving the day. There is a ram in the thicket. There is a suitable substitute.

As the cross is the intersection of God's mercy and wrath, the altar of Isaac is the intersection of Abraham's faith and sin. This is a template for God's offering of his only Son, of course, but it's not an easy one; it is not a one-to-one correlation. Abraham is making an offering for his sin—God has no sin; he makes the offering for ours. But to atone for his sin, Abraham is asked to offer his son, a more painful sacrifice than if he were asked to offer up himself. Until the ram is revealed, Abraham is suffering the God-sanctioned despair of his own sin and the God-echoed sadness over the loss of his own son. The connection between this story and Calvary is deeper than it appears at first glance, more complex. God is an artist.

This story is a fountain into the Old Testament, its flow spilling in all directions, tributaries of blood running forward and back. The fountain is spring-fed by the Gospels, the resulting river running wide in the far east of Genesis 22 and terminating as far west as Revelation 12:11: "And they have conquered him by the blood of the Lamb and by the word of their testimony, for they loved not their lives even unto death." In Revelation 22, the river of blood gives way to a crystal stream. It has always been life, but where it once looked like death, it will then gleam with the glory of the imperishable.

When I say the story of Abraham, Isaac, and God's provision is a fountain that flows everywhere into the Old Testament, what I mean is that this story finds itself foreshadowed and aftershocked in the myriad threads of God's dealings with his covenant people. The need for atonement, the desire for atonement, and the alien provision of atonement is the true story of God and man. If we get this right, we will get the gospel right.

We ought never disregard, diminish, or discard that knife hovering over the bound son. If we lose its sharpness, we lose all else that comes through his wounds. As Martin Hengel says, "The spearhead cannot be broken off the spear."[2]

THE SHARP SHORTHAND

The biblical gospel is a multidimensional, full-orbed gospel. It is deep. That is the premise of this book. But there is also a fine point to it, this sharpness at hand, and we see it in the way the apostles shorthanded their message. The cross was at the center of their proclamation. Paul references the gospel as "the word of the cross" (1 Cor. 1:18). He doesn't boast in anything "except in the cross" (Gal. 6:14). He preaches "Christ crucified" (1 Cor. 1:23).

Is he shortchanging the resurrection? No, this is shorthand, and it is summed up in the fine point of the gospel message: the cross. This biblical summation is in mind in the best of what is called "cross-centered writing." Responding to critics of the descriptor "cross-centered," Jeff Purswell writes:

> I don't think any of us would want our doctrine diluted down to a single adjective. However, this particular phrase reflects a common New Testament pattern in which "the cross" functions as shorthand for all the various facets of Christ's atoning work—life, death, resurrection, and ascension.[3]

---

[2] Martin Hengel, *Crucifixion in the Ancient World and the Folly of the Message of the Cross* (Philadelphia: Fortress, 1977), 90.
[3] Jeff Purswell, "Will Focusing on the Cross Lead Us to Neglect the Resurrection?" C. J.'s *View from the Cheap Seats* (blog), August 25, 2010, http://sovereigngraceministries.org/blogs/cj-mahaney/

Why does the cross function as suitable shorthand for the deep gospel? Because it is the fulcrum upon which the entire story of redemption turns. Yes, there is no salvation without the resurrection, but there is no resurrection without the crucifixion, and as we have seen, it is the crucifixion which the Old Testament anticipates most vividly. (The resurrection of the Messiah is back there too, undoubtedly, but as the surprise twist in the story, it is more artfully concealed in that first act.[4]) And it is the crucifixion that serves as the sharp shorthand for the gospel's announcement in the epistles of the New Testament.[5]

THE "–ATIONS" OF THE CROSS

As the gospel is deep, the cross itself carries depths and dimensions, as well. If we take a look at the variety of sacrifices prescribed in the Old Testament, we will see that Jesus satisfies this variety through the single offering of himself. We see the dimensions of his accomplishment in what I call the –ations of the cross. No, not the stations of the cross. The –ations. To wit:

Mediation. There is a gulf between us and God, held in tension by his justified wrath owed to us for our sin. At the cross, the sinless Christ bridges the void between us and God by covering our sin, establishing the foundation for his future, ongoing mediation between us and God in his work as advocate and intercessor (1 John 2:1; Heb. 7:25).

Condemnation. We have a true and better mediator than Moses or any priest because Christ the Mediator stands in the place of the condemned, not just handling our sin but taking it upon himself as the object of sacrifice. He accepts the place of the guilty in order to exchange his innocence. Therefore he goes to the cross willingly, because it is the foreordained place of condemnation where we all belong. He becomes the substitute condemned.

Propitiation. A blood debt is owed, legally speaking, because without the shedding of blood there can be no forgiveness of sins,

---

post/2010/08/25/1-Will-focusing-on-the-cross-lead-us-to-neglect-the-resurrection.aspx.
[4] See Psalm 16:10; Hosea 6:1–2; and of course "the sign of Jonah," among others.
[5] See John Stott's masterful treatment of this position in the chapter titled "The Centrality of the Cross" in his *The Cross of Christ* (Downer's Grove, IL: InterVarsity, 2006), 23–50.

and until the price is paid the condemned remain under the justified wrath of God. We cannot make this payment because we have no currency with which to do so. We are morally bankrupt, every last one of us. So at the cross, Christ makes satisfaction, fulfilling this payment with the riches of himself, supplying his life to take the debt upon himself and thereby appeasing and averting the wrath of God. The result of Christ's propitiation is that God is "made favorable" toward us.

Justification. Nearly all of Christ's crosswork put together merits what we receive through faith: right standing before God. Because of the cross, where Jesus's perfect obedience culminates in and effects his perfect sacrifice, we receive a full pardon. We for whom there was no justification are now justified.

Imputation. There is a crediting to accounts, both ways. At the cross, Christ takes the sin out of our account and puts it into his as he becomes the condemned on the cross, but in doing *that*, he transfers his innocence to the account of those actually guilty. Our sin is imputed to him as if it were his, and his righteousness is imputed to us as if it were ours. "For our sake he made him to be sin who knew no sin, so that in him we might become the righteousness of God" (2 Cor. 5:21).

Expiation. But Jesus doesn't stop there. With his life given sacrificially on the cross, he doesn't just take on our debt, he eradicates it completely. The work of expiation is the radical cleansing of the guilty from sin.

> For if the blood of goats and bulls, and the sprinkling of defiled persons with the ashes of a heifer, sanctify for the purification of the flesh, how much more will the blood of Christ, who through the eternal Spirit offered himself without blemish to God, purify our conscience from dead works to serve the living God. (Heb. 9:13–14)

In Christ's expiating work, we are purified—not just declared righteous, but purified spiritually into righteousness.

Sanctification. This is an ongoing work of the Spirit, to be sure, but thanks to Christ's expiating work on the cross, we are also definitively sanctified on the cross, which is to say, cleansed by his blood (1 Cor. 6:11). The initial sanctification then and even the ongoing sanctification now are the effects of the cross-cause, the outworking of our justification.

Reconciliation. And since we are justified before God, we are reconciled to him. The gulf is bridged, the wrath appeased, the debt canceled and cast into the void, the soul cleansed. Christ's wide-open arms at the cross reveal to us the means of the Father embracing his once-lost children. Through the cross, Christ reconciles us to God (Col. 1:20).

Nations. Who is Christ's crosswork for, exactly (1 John 2:2)?

These are but the highest peaks of the atonement's mountainous surface. Jesus has done so much! But there is a fine point to these points, a concept into which they converge and from which they protrude. At each of these points, we see that Christ is standing in our place, doing what we ought to do but cannot do.

As the cross is the center of the gospel, penal substitution is the center of the cross.

IN MY PLACE CONDEMNED HE STOOD

Penal substitution is the sharp edge of the atonement.[6] It is not all that is Christ's atoning work, but everything else the atonement *is* is brought through in the wake of penal substitution's lead, as a thread is pulled by a needle.

There are several views of the atonement, sometimes called "theories," some true and some not. Penal substitution's twin is *Christus Victor*, the view of the atonement that sees Christ's work on the cross as the defeat of the forces of evil and the subjection of death to his sovereign lordship. John Knox—the twentieth-century seminary professor, not the sixteenth-century Scottish Reformer—pairs them in this claim: "a victory won [and] a sacrifice offered . . . belong to the very warp and woof of the New Testament."[7]

---

[6] "Penal" because it envisions penalty-taking; "substitution" because it envisions the punishment deserved by one as taken by another. "For Christ also suffered once for sins, the righteous for the unrighteous, that he might bring us to God, being put to death in the flesh but made alive in the spirit" (1 Pet. 3:18).

[7] John Knox, *The Death of Christ: The Cross in New Testament History and Faith* (New York: Abingdon, 1958), 146.

Christus Victor, like penal substitution, is not a theory; it is—*they are*—the truth. But penal substitution is the twin born first. There is no victory over sin and death until the wages are paid, and these are not paid to anyone but the one authorized to condemn, the one against whom sin is an offense. The offended Holy One, then, owes condemnation to those who have fallen short of his glory, and the victory of his glory is accomplished through the pouring out of that condemnation onto a substitutionary sacrifice—in the old covenant the various sacrificial offerings, in the new covenant the one offering of Christ. Even Gustaf Aulén, who most influentially showed us the Christus Victor view in the writings of the church fathers, writes that Christus Victor is "juridical in its inmost essence."[8]

Some more lately have controversially argued that penal substitution is not evident among the views of the church fathers. Others, equally controversially, have demonstrated that it is.[9] It is outside the scope of this work to survey antiquity for support of penal substitution's historical credibility, as others have already clearly done that, but as part of our reveling in the depths of the gospel, we will survey along with them the biblical logic for the centrality of the view.

We find in John's Gospel, for instance, a revelation of Christ's multifaceted glory, but the substitutionary atonement holds the facets together. Let's take a walk through the book to sense its main point. Jesus is, in this one book, the Bread of Life, the Light of the World, the Door, the Good Shepherd, the Resurrection, the Life, the Vine, and so on. But the through-line of John's Gospel is Jesus the sacrificial Lamb. As the Gospel opens, John the Baptist is echoing (and fulfilling) Isaiah—"I am the voice of one crying out in the wilderness, 'Make straight the way of the Lord'" (John 1:23; see Isa. 40:3)—in a gospel announcement drawn straight from a prophecy of pardon:

---

[8]Gustaf Aulén, *Christus Victor*, trans. A. G. Hebert (London: SPCK, 1931), 106. Quoted in J. I. Packer, "The Logic of Penal Substitution" (Tyndale Biblical Theology Lecture, Tyndale House, Cambridge, UK, July 17, 1973), http://www.the-highway.com/cross_Packer.html.
[9]See most notably Steve Jeffery, Michael Ovey, and Andrew Sach, *Pierced for Our Transgressions: Rediscovering the Glory of Penal Substitution* (Wheaton, IL: Crossway, 2007). Also, Michael J. Vlach, "Penal Substitution in Church History," *The Master's Seminary Journal*, 20, no. 2 (Fall 2009): 199–214.

Comfort, comfort my people, says your God.
Speak tenderly to Jerusalem,
> and cry to her
that her warfare is ended,
> that her iniquity is pardoned,
that she has received from the LORD's hand
> double for all her sins. (Isa. 40:1–2)

As if on cue, his cousin Jesus approaches, prompting John to declare, "Behold, the Lamb of God, who takes away the sin of the world!" (John 1:29). He says it again (in John 1:35), drawing the first disciples. Thus John's Gospel begins with penal substitution in the foreground.

In John 2:13–22, Jesus cryptically shares that the destruction of his body will substitute for the cleansing of the temple's corruption in judgment. In John 3:14–15, Jesus compares the lifting up of his body on the cross to the uplifted Mosaic serpent that absorbed the impending death from all who looked upon it. In John 3:16–21, we learn that Jesus has come in God's love to take away the condemnation of God's wrath deserved by sinful man. John 3:36 says, "Whoever believes in the Son has eternal life; whoever does not obey the Son shall not see life, but the wrath of God remains on him." In John 5:24, Jesus says that whoever believes in the Son will be saved from God's judgment. John 5:45 brings into play the legal court language of God's commands via Moses, where the need for penal substitution is right at home. If we may include the woman caught in adultery (7:53–8:11) as original to John's Gospel, we see that Jesus, in an ominous foreshadow of his execution, stands in for the woman who is about to be stoned and pardons her condemnation. In John 9:35–41, Jesus says that he came into the world "for judgment" of the blind, that they will see. In John 12:12–15, the crowd cries from Zechariah upon Jesus's triumphal entry into Jerusalem, quoting a passage (Zech. 9:9–13) that contains God's promising salvation by the blood of the covenant (9:11). In John 12:44–50, Jesus says he came to save the world from judgment.

The pace quickens as John's story rises to crescendo upon the commemoration of the Passover, where the blood of the lamb saved God's children from his wrath. Jesus brings up the ramifications of the Law again in John 15:18–25 and himself as the satisfaction of its demands. In the middle of his high priestly prayer, Jesus says to the Father, "And for their sake I consecrate myself, that they also may be sanctified in truth" (17:19), asserting himself in death as the means of our being made holy. In 18:39–40, Jesus is substituted for Barabbas, a robber who legally deserves execution for his sin. The crucifixion of Jesus coincides with the time of Passover.

So we see that John's Gospel, which of all the biblical books is one of the heaviest proclamations of God's love and one of the most cosmic, nuanced, and multileveled perspectives of Christ's vocation, has as its leitmotif and logical pivot the presentation of Christ as sacrifice in the absorption of God's judgment on sinful man. This is but one example.

As the New Testament expounds on the multitudinous glories of Christ's atoning work—ransoming prisoners, liberating slaves, conquering the Devil, killing sin, uniting believers, exemplifying goodness, healing sickness—it remains through all tethered to the satisfying of God's holy wrath legally owed to sinners for the "cosmic treason" against his glory.[10]

Returning to Knox, we read, "As helpless sinners (which we are) we need *deliverance*. As responsible sinners (which we also are) we need *forgiveness*."[11] Jesus saves us from many things. We are truly victims of sin, but we're also the perpetrators. We don't just suffer evil; we produce it. We *are* it. Therefore, the gospel's announcement of salvation is fundamentally salvation from the wrath of God.

"Christ redeemed us from the curse of the law by becoming a curse for us," we find in Galatians 3:13. "Since, therefore, we have now been justified by his blood, much more shall we be saved by him from the wrath of God," rejoices Romans 5:9. Jesus has delivered us from the wrath to come, Paul writes in 1 Thessalonians 1:10. We who "were by nature children of wrath, like the rest of

---

[10] R. C. Sproul, *The Holiness of God* (Carol Stream, IL: Tyndale, 1998), 116.
[11] John Knox, *The Death of Christ: The Cross in New Testament History and Faith* (New York: Abingdon, 1958), 152.

mankind" were made alive with Christ Jesus, "even when we were dead in our trespasses" (Eph. 2:3–5).

First Corinthians 15 is one of the most vivid "Christus Victor" treatises, but as Christ is victor, as Christ is reigning, as Christ is putting all things in subjection to himself, as Christ is purchasing our future resurrection to share in his glorification, we see that the linchpin for all this earth-encompassing goodness and glory is that "Christ died for our sins in accordance with the Scriptures" (15:3)—by which we take it to mean in accordance with the Law's demand for, the history's foreshadow of, and the prophets' forecast of atonement by blood—and that he has taken the sting of death to satisfy the demand of the law (15:56).

Penal substitution is all over the New Testament, but is plainly taught by Paul in his letter to the Romans. Here is the tip of the knife that is the entire epistle:

> For all have sinned and fall short of the glory of God, and are justified by his grace as a gift, through the redemption that is in Christ Jesus, whom God put forward as a propitiation by his blood, to be received by faith. This was to show God's righteousness, because in his divine forbearance he had passed over former sins. It was to show his righteousness at the present time, so that he might be just and the justifier of the one who has faith in Jesus. (Rom. 3:23–26)

There is debate over the meaning of the Greek behind what the ESV has translated here as *propitiation*, and I will leave that debate to better minds than mine, but whether expiation or propitiation—whether Jesus as propitiating lamb or expiating scapegoat—is in view here, we see that Christ's sacrificial offering is the vehicle of God's "forbearing" judgment and "passing over" of sins. Of this passage Cranfield writes:

> We take it that what Paul's statement that God purposed Christ as a propitiatory victim means is that God, because in His mercy He willed to forgive sinful men and, being truly merciful, willed to forgive them righteously, that is, without in any way condoning their sin, purposed to direct against His own very Self in the

person of His Son the full weight of that righteous wrath which they deserved.[12]

The presence of sin makes us many things: slaves, hungry, dead, etc., and Christ's cross cures these ills, but at the door to the room of this variegated antidote is a check for the right to enter, and only penal substitution provides that right.

THE COVENANT NARRATIVE AND PENAL SUBSTITUTION

In Edgar Allan Poe's classic tale "The Purloined Letter," the titular missive is missed, but not for lack of ransacking the house. Turns out that it remained safe immediately under the detectives' noses, hanging from a card rack in the midst of the ravaged room, protected by its visibility. Many scholars claim to have looked and looked into God's Word for penal substitution and come up empty-handed. Like Poe's purloined letter, somehow penal substitution has managed to hide from them in plain sight.

Echoing Knox, Bruce Demarest writes, "The idea of vicarious, penal substitution is imbedded in the warp and woof of Scripture."[13] As we have seen, the river of Christ's blood runs throughout the Scriptures. The blood splatter from the murder of Jesus lands as far back as Genesis 3:21: "And the LORD God made for Adam and for his wife garments of skins and clothed them."

Adam and Eve had clothed themselves with fig leaves, a pathetic covering for their shame. One may perhaps see the seed of Cain's produce offering here; but the fruit of human labor is no justification for spiritual death. Death in, death out. Something has to die. So God covers them in animal skins.

The sacrifices begin as early as Genesis 4. Abel's offering of the slaughtered firstborn of his sheep flock is offered in faith, and God accepts it.

God establishes his covenant with Abraham by cutting him. This is serious business. Then he promises Abraham the son Isaac,

---

[12] Charles E. B. Cranfield, *A Critical and Exegetical Commentary on the Epistle to the Romans* (Edinburgh: T&T Clark, 1975), 1:217.
[13] Bruce Demarest, *The Cross and Salvation: The Doctrine of Salvation* (Wheaton, IL: Crossway, 1997), 171.

and we have already seen how Isaac's story foretells the sacrificial offering of Jesus.

The bloodshed continues, and the Passover is the most vivid example. Here God brings wrath, but those who in faith have painted the blood of the lamb over their doorway are saved. The Passover leads directly into the climactic Exodus event, a mythic (which is not to say unhistorical) connection that finds its completion in Christ's crucifixion, giving way to his resurrection and his deliverance into heaven, and ours. In the crossing of the Red Sea, the drowning of the Egyptians, and the Israelite flight into the wilderness, we see command and conquest—we see Christus Victor—but in the preceding Passover we see penal substitution.

The book of Leviticus is a catalog of sacrificial prescriptions. A variety of offerings represent a variety of emphases—cleanliness, unity, worship, expiation, propitiation—but the sum of the system is justification of sinners to a holy God. Warfield tracks the through-line:

> It is not to be doubted, of course, that elements of adoration and of sacramental communion also enter into the sacrificial rites of the Levitical system: nothing could be clearer than that in the several sacrificial ordinances, a variety of religious motives find appropriate expression, and a variety of religious impressions are aimed at and produced. But it would seem quite impossible to erect these motives and impressions into the main, and certainly not into the sole, notion expressed or object sought in these ordinances. It may be confidently contended that, present as they undoubtedly are, they are present as subsidiary and ancillary to the fundamental function of the sacrifice, which is to propitiate the offended deity in behalf of sinful man. Any unbiased study of the Levitical system must issue, as it seems to us, in the conviction that this system is through and through, in its intention and effect, piacular.[14]

The sacrifices of animals are most obviously so. Harrison adds:

[14] Benjamin B. Warfield, "Christ Our Sacrifice," in *The Works of Benjamin B. Warfield*, vol. 2, *Biblical Doctrines* (Grand Rapids, MI: Baker, 2003), 423.

In view of the consistent Old Testament tradition that sin was a most serious matter in God's sight, and merited the most drastic punishment, it is difficult to see how the slain sacrifices could be interpreted in any other than penal terms, with the animal acting as a substitute for the sinner.[15]

Leviticus 17:11 dials us in: "For the life of the flesh is in the blood, and I have given it for you on the altar to make atonement for your souls, for it is the blood that makes atonement by the life." Hamilton will round out the scholarly survey:

> The regulations set forth in Leviticus are a judgment, and they make it possible for people to substitute animals of sacrifice that will be judged in their place, that they might be saved. . . . Leviticus adds that Israel herself is sinful and must seek atonement for sin through substitutionary sacrifice that appeases the wrath of God. Thus may Yahweh justly show mercy. The penal substitutionary sacrifices are demanded by the very glory of God.[16]

The Levitical Day of Atonement arcs through the generations, landing on Golgotha. The sacrifices commanded in Leviticus pour into the rest of the old covenant narrative. God's people are unfaithful, but God is faithful. God's people are unholy, but God is holy. God's people take his name in vain, but God is jealous for his name, that it be kept holy. So the blood continues to flow, and as the threat of calamity and collapse reverberate back upon every disobedience to the covenant, God nevertheless promises mercy, a day of deliverance. In the shadows lurks Israel's salvific substitute.

Judges 19:22–30, recounting the rape and murder of the concubine, is one of the most horrific texts in all the Bible. Plugging the reference into Google reveals it is used by many haters of the faith as examples of the Bible's awfulness and unreliability. And the passage *does* reveal something awful. What do we do with something like this?

The first thing we need to say is that the Bible contains many

---

[15] R. K. Harrison, *Leviticus*, Tyndale Old Testament Commentary (Downer's Grove, IL: Inter-Varsity, 1980), 182.
[16] James M. Hamilton Jr., *God's Glory in Salvation through Judgment: A Biblical Theology* (Wheaton, IL: Crossway, 2010), 114.

passages that are descriptive, and this does not make them prescriptive. Contrary to what many of the online opponents of biblical authority would have us think, there is no approval from God for the man of Gibeah's heinous bargain or the subsequent rape, murder, and mutilation of the concubine. The Levite gives up his concubine as some sort of trade of self-protection. And that the concubine's dismembered body is grotesquely sent around Israel is reacted to the way it ought to be: notice that the people's reaction is shock. "Such a thing has never happened or been seen from the day that the people of Israel came up out of the land of Egypt until this day," they say (Judg. 19:30).

A woman in my church asked me how an unsaved person might read this passage in the Bible; she was concerned that unbelievers might think the Bible is somehow condoning this act. But we'd have to show them otherwise. The gruesome event is in fact a consequence of everyone's doing what was right in their own eyes (17:6; 21:25), a consequence of having no king over Israel (19:1). Judges 19:22–30 shows that the Bible is honest and realistic about the depravity of man when left to his own devices. Further, the punch of the narrative is that what was thought only to happen among the pagans was now happening in the heartland of Israel at the hands of God's people. Judges 19 drives the guilt of sin home and places it in every heart. Judges 19 is honest; it is not putting a gloss on what men are capable of, which we can clearly see on the evening news. And while we should be disgusted by the imagery, we should also commend the Bible's brutal honesty.

But there is a gospel spring beneath this text too. When there is no king in Israel, men betray their women. A woman is unprotected and given over to enemies to have their way with her, and then she is made an example of in a murderous way to the twelve tribes. But when Jesus is King over Israel, he protects his bride; he won't give her over to the enemy to have his way with her. And Jesus leaves the house himself and offers his own body, going in his bride's stead to be torn apart for the twelve tribes of Israel. Instead of giving us up in some evil bargain, he gives himself up. And his battered body is the sign to his people that he won't sell them out.

Jesus suffers this kind of sin in absorbing the wrath for this kind of sin in order to forgive this kind of sin.

In Psalm 22 David is a placeholder for the forsaken Son of God who nevertheless accomplishes God's righteousness.

Isaiah 53 contains the most direct Old Testament depiction of Christ's penal substitution:

> Surely he has borne our griefs
>   and carried our sorrows;
> yet we esteemed him stricken,
>   smitten by God, and afflicted.
> But he was pierced for our transgressions;
>   he was crushed for our iniquities;
> upon him was the chastisement that brought us peace,
>   and with his stripes we are healed.
> All we like sheep have gone astray;
>   we have turned—every one—to his own way;
> and the LORD has laid on him
>   the iniquity of us all.
> He was oppressed, and he was afflicted,
>   yet he opened not his mouth;
> like a lamb that is led to the slaughter,
>   and like a sheep that before its shearers is silent,
>   so he opened not his mouth.
> By oppression and judgment he was taken away;
>   and as for his generation, who considered
> that he was cut off out of the land of the living,
>   stricken for the transgression of my people?
> And they made his grave with the wicked
>   and with a rich man in his death,
> although he had done no violence,
>   and there was no deceit in his mouth.
> Yet it was the will of the LORD to crush him;
>   he has put him to grief;
> when his soul makes an offering for guilt,
>   he shall see his offspring; he shall prolong his days;
> the will of the LORD shall prosper in his hand.
> Out of the anguish of his soul he shall see and be satisfied;
> by his knowledge shall the righteous one, my servant,
>   make many to be accounted righteous,

and he shall bear their iniquities.
Therefore I will divide him a portion with the many,
    and he shall divide the spoil with the strong,
because he poured out his soul to death
    and was numbered with the transgressors;
yet he bore the sin of many,
    and makes intercession for the transgressors. (Isa. 53:4–12)

The other covenant prophets keep sounding the alarm of God's coming judgment . . . and God's coming deliverance. There is no mistaking the crossroads they are foretelling.

Peter picks up this narrative in Acts 2, warning in his gospel proclamation that the peril of Hades is unavoidable for those who have not repented and called upon the name of the Lord to be saved.

As the early church grows, the apostles preach again and again the covenant narrative as cross-shaped. The specter of Deuteronomy 21:22–23 looms over the Jews' grappling with the crucifixion:

> And if a man has committed a crime punishable by death and he is put to death, and you hang him on a tree, his body shall not remain all night on the tree, but you shall bury him the same day, for a hanged man is cursed by God. You shall not defile your land that the LORD your God is giving you for an inheritance.

Peter and Paul make it a point to arouse this specter in their gospel preaching (Acts 5:30; 10:39; 13:29; Gal. 3:13; 1 Pet. 2:24).

And when the covenant story reaches its crescendo in the book of Revelation, Christ comes in wrath. But not for those on whose behalf he has already received it at the cross.

THE CUP AND ITS WINE

We cannot pit God's love and his wrath against each other, as if wrath must give way as superstition, or we stand damned like Marcion. Brunner warns: "Where the idea of the wrath of God is ignored, there also will there be no understanding of the central conception of the Gospel."[17]

---

[17] Emil Brunner, *The Mediator*, trans. Olive Wyon (Philadelphia: Westminster, 1947), 152; quoted in John Stott, *The Cross of Christ* (Downers Grove, IL: InterVarsity, 2006), 111.

As the cross is the center of the gospel, so penal substitution is the center of the cross.

The caricature of Christ's taking the wrath of God as cosmic child abuse fails to grasp Jesus's own words about his sacrifice and ultimately the Trinitarian economy, where there is equality of essence and authority but also of glory-reflecting and deference. The caricature also fails to wrestle with the deep, deep love of God. As we noted in chapter 1, to "reconcile" God's love and God's wrath into the oblivion of one or the other does not do justice to God's bigness at all. It is a woeful flattening.

We may face these depths perhaps nowhere more substantively than in Jesus's tormented night in the garden of Gethsemane. Jesus, prostrate and sorrowful unto death, prays, "My Father, if it be possible, let this cup pass from me; nevertheless, not as I will, but as you will" (Matt. 26:39). Luke tells us that Jesus is sweating blood (Luke 22:44).

What do we make of this?

First, there is no mistaking this "cup." It is throughout the covenant narrative representative of nothing less than God's wrath. Its pouring out is repeatedly forewarned. Psalm 11:4. Isaiah 51:17. Jeremiah 25. Ezekiel 23:31–34. Habakkuk 2:16. Revelation 14:10 and 16:19.

In the garden, Jesus knows he is about to succumb to the swallowing up of all that the cross is, a terrible baptism (Mark 10:38–39; Luke 12:50). The tannins of Christ's blood contain many hints and strains, a variety of atonement blessings, but they are all pressed forth through God's wrathful crushing. When the wrath of God is satisfied, the penalty is paid and therefore the victory is secured and his love is fulfilled.

"Not my will," Jesus says, because he loves his Father and he loves those given him by the Father. "Your will," Jesus says, because he knows that the satisfaction of God's wrath is the ultimate manifestation of God's love.

Rebecca Pippert writes, "The lessons of the cross are ones we never outgrow, for the further we go the deeper we get."[18] If we

---

[18] Rebecca Pippert, *Hope Has Its Reasons* (New York: Harper & Row, 1989), 159.

would sense this depth, and revel in it, if we would taste the sweetness of God's atoning work in Christ, we must acquire a taste for the bitterness, for the atonement's sharpness. Like Isaiah's atonement in the temple, we will find the sting on our lips a liberating bliss. In his poem "The Agonie," George Herbert conveys the ecstasy thusly:

> Philosophers have measur'd mountains,
> Fathom'd the depths of seas, of states, and kings,
> Walk'd with a staff to heav'n, and traced fountains:
> But there are two vast, spacious things,
> The which to measure it doth more behove:
> Yet few there are that sound them; Sinne and Love.
>
> Who would know Sinne, let him repair
> Unto Mount Olivet; there shall he see
> A man so wrung with pains, that all his hair,
> His skinne, his garments bloudie be.
> Sinne is that press and vice, which forceth pain
> To hunt his cruel food through ev'ry vein.
>
> Who knows not Love, let him assay
> And taste that juice, which on the crosse a pike
> Did set again abroach; then let him say
> If ever he did taste the like.
> Love is that liquor sweet and most divine,
> Which my God feels as bloud; but I, as wine.[19]

At the cross, God's wrath is satisfied. Atonement is made. "There is therefore now no condemnation for those who are in Christ Jesus" (Rom. 8:1).

One reason we must center on the penal aspect of the cross is so that, in our pondering of our persistent sin in the light of God's holiness, we do not gravely mistake temporal suffering for the wrath of God. What (and why) suffering is, and how the gospel applies to it, will be the focus of our next chapter.

---

[19] George Herbert, "The Agonie," in *The Essential Herbert*, selected by Anthony Hecht (New York: Ecco Press, 1987), 25

Chapter Six

THE GLORY OF SUFFERING

"The King keeps his best wine
in the cellar of affliction."
—attributed to Samuel Rutherford

The question is universal. As a pastor, I not only ask it but receive it. Constantly. It is this: "If God is good, why does he allow such suffering?"

As I write this chapter I have an e-mail in my in-box from a reader of my blog who is, by her own admission, not a Christian but, in her words, "wants to be." But she cannot understand why God would create some people knowing they would never accept him and will go to hell. She understands that to believe the Bible is to believe what it teaches about the eternal conscious torment of unrepentant sinners. She knows she must go "all in" on that doctrine. She will not play games with it. She is not asking that it be mitigated, dismissed, or metaphored away to make the faith more palatable to her. Nevertheless, it is a sticking point for her. She wants to know, given this teaching, why Christianity ought to be palatable to her.

As often as I answer this question, I still feel as though I'm starting from scratch each time I give it a go. I have to ask myself the question each time as well, and relearn afresh God's purposes in the allowance of suffering. I have a fear of sounding like one of Job's stupid friends. So I have put off responding to this lady until I can answer as a helpful friend and fellow searcher for solace, rather than as an advice-giving "expert."

One initial comfort we may receive is just in knowing that the Scriptures don't ignore the reality and the complexity of pain. Some religions hold that suffering is just an illusion, others that it can be easily conquered through mind control. God's revealed

Word, on the other hand, deals in truth. The Psalms, for instance, show us many things, among them the complicated depths and various shades of human suffering. Physical, psychological, emotional, spiritual. As Calvin says, the Psalms are "an anatomy of all the parts of the soul."[1] Sin and its earned curse have spread like a cancer, seeping into every earthen nook and cranny. And so the human soul suffers in a variety of ways, and the Bible is not ignorant of this.

I met for coffee recently with a dear friend and member of my church who has been out of work for a long time. He is struggling to make ends meet and is underwater on his mortgage. He can't get hired in his field because nobody is hiring; he can't get hired outside his field because nobody's hiring, or he's considered overqualified. Unemployment benefits are barely beneficial, but he doesn't feel comfortable accepting them anyway. He wants to work. On top of all that, he, his wife, and one of his children have struggled off and on over the last year with illnesses and other ongoing health scares. One of their vehicles became inoperable. A windstorm blew his fence down, snapping the posts in half. A few hours after I met with him, his wife came home and discovered their house had been robbed.

What is happening? They cried, "Uncle!" a long time ago.

The stress is weighing on my friend. His family is depending on him, and despite his honorable desire to do honest work for honest pay, despite his family's desire to order their lives around God's Word and steward all things for his glory, God appears to be holding out on them.

"Why can't we catch a break? Where is God in this?" he asks. "Why wouldn't God allow me to do the right thing? I'm not trying to be rich. The Bible says if a man will not work, he will not eat. The Bible says a man who does not provide for his family is worse than an unbeliever. Why won't God let me obey these rules?"

At this very moment, Christians with the same feelings as you and me are facing execution in the Middle East and Asia for their

---

[1] John Calvin, *Commentary on the Book of Psalms*, trans. James Anderson (Edinburgh, UK: Calvin Translation Society, 1845), 1:xxxvii.

faith. They will be asked to recant (or return to the faith of their fathers), and they will refuse. They will already have been beaten. Headlines in the West about our brothers and sisters remind us that "taking up your cross" still means in some nations what it did in Jesus's.

We all have friends who are recovering from abuse or living with chronic pain or grieving the loss of a loved one. Or we are those friends.

In the time it took me to write the previous paragraphs, approximately 150 babies under four weeks of age died worldwide of preventable causes.

A world of experience awaits every soul, and thus a world of suffering.

Why does God let this happen?

The short answer is, "We don't know."

We really don't know. When Job is questioning God about his suffering, God does not offer Job "Chicken Soup for the Soul," but takes him straight into the disorienting depths of his might and sovereignty. He answers with a heady dose of perspective, an epic and poetic extrapolation of Isaiah 55:8:

> For my thoughts are not your thoughts,
>   neither are your ways my ways, declares the LORD.

That verse has been trotted out so much we have come to treat it like a cliché, a dodge of some inconvenient theological questions, but if it ever suited an inquiry, this is the one.

The Bible talks about suffering a lot, and it gives us some reasons why God allows suffering, but it doesn't put us inside his mind in the sense of providing that silver-bullet rationale. Our motives are not entirely pure, however. What many of us are really asking when we say "Why would God allow this to happen?" is "Why won't God justify himself according to my perspective on how the world should be run?"

Nevertheless, *why* can be a good and honest question, and it is certainly a natural and understandable one. It reveals what we all know deep down: this world is not as it should be.

The alleviation of suffering is a good thing. The Christian Church ought to take up that mantle as a missional charge in the world, for God's glory and as a testimony to his love. But in the end, we are faced with two biblical realities we may not be able to fully reconcile until we know as we are known. The first is this: suffering happens. The second is this: God is good.

Those realities appear to run parallel tracks for many, including the lady whose e-mail is burning a hole in my in-box. But the Bible gives us an abundance of clues about how *and where* suffering and the goodness of God intersect. We have to say, "I don't know," as it pertains to the mind of God, but he has not been stingy with answers to the *why* question in what he has revealed.

WHY DOES GOD ALLOW SUFFERING?

The Scriptures may not put us inside God's higher harmonizing of his goodness and the world's pervasive evil, but they do speak to God's purposes in suffering quite a bit. In fact, while we may not be satisfied with what God has revealed about his purposes in suffering, we cannot justifiably say he has not revealed anything about his purposes in suffering. We may not have the answer we are laboring for, but we do have a wealth of answers that lie in the same field.

Why, according to God's Word, does God allow suffering?

1. *To remind us that the world is broken and groans for redemption.* Paul writes in Romans 8:20–23:

> For the creation was subjected to futility, not willingly, but because of him who subjected it, in hope that the creation itself will be set free from its bondage to corruption and obtain the freedom of the glory of the children of God. For we know that the whole creation has been groaning together in the pains of childbirth until now. And not only the creation, but we ourselves.

The presence of suffering in the world, and the conditions that give rise to it—from disease to natural disasters, social injustice to personal evil—serve as a constant signal that this place is messed up. The whole creation is groaning, longing to be freed from the curse of the fall. God allows suffering, then, so that we will know we need deliverance from a fallen world.

2. *To do justice in response to Adam's (and our) sin.* God has allowed suffering as the natural consequence of Adam and Eve's disobedience. The rebellion was severer than severe; therefore, there is no escape this side of heaven from the reach of the curse. The suffering that exists in the world is a result of man's original cosmic treason against God.

Now, this sense of justice is not to be seen in the same way as *punishment*. In other words, you did not get cancer because God is punishing you for some specific sin or set of sins. Jesus himself comes against this sort of idea in John 9:1–3, when he denies that the man born blind had received his condition due to his sin or the sin of his parents. In Luke 13:1–5, Jesus further disconnects the reality of suffering from punishment for sin. And of course one of the first things we learn about Job is that he is "blameless and upright" (Job 1:1), singled out for temptation precisely *because* God sees him as righteous.

Nevertheless, while pain and suffering are not always a punishment for sin (we should not rule out that pain sometimes is the direct result of sin, as in the case of capital punishment or someone's defense of self against assault or illnesses brought on by substance abuse, but those aren't typically what's envisioned in questions of human suffering), they are the consequences of original and continuing sinfulness in the world, the curse placed on the world because of the fall. Childbirth and work are not bad things, and the pain and toil they entail are not direct recompense for personal sins, but in Genesis 3 we learn that pain in childbirth and toilsome sweat in work are part of God's retributive justice for Adam and Eve's disobedience.

3. *To remind us of the severity of the impact of Adam's (and our) sin.* Not only is the presence of pain and suffering a work of justice in response to Adam and Eve's rebellion, but the severity of pain and suffering remind us of the severity of sin's rebellion against God. His holiness is a precious thing, and a crime against it is an awful

thing. The depths of human suffering in this world, while not a direct punishment for an individual sufferer's sins, nevertheless show us just how deep the enmity Adam created between man and God is.

4. *To keep us dependent on God.* As I was counseling a man going through severe circumstantial difficulties, I asked him, "If these things weren't happening in your life, would you be as close to God as you are right now?" He admitted that he likely would not. When I was going through the dark period of rejection, depression, and despair that gave way to gospel wakefulness, I realized that God would become my only hope only when he had become my only hope. (Let the reader understand.)

In a similar way to how uncertainty and a lack of control provoke in us the faith that God requires from us, pain and suffering provoke in us the utter dependence on God that he requires from us. If we look at life biblically, comfort is actually the illusion this side of heaven, not pain. When things are going well, the temptation is greater to neglect our devotion to God. We don't feel our need for him, so we don't express it.

The author of Hebrews writes:

> "For the Lord disciplines the one he loves,
>   and chastises every son whom he receives."

> It is for discipline that you have to endure. God is treating you as sons. For what son is there whom his father does not discipline? (Heb. 12:6–7)

Again, the discipline in mind here is not punishment. It is more along the lines of "training." God keeps us close to him by allowing the pain of this world to direct us to our need. Like a good shepherd, he keeps us close to him with the rod of affliction.

5. *So that we will long more for heaven and less for the world.* The pain and suffering abundant in this world push us to seek our abundance elsewhere. They help us to groan for the redemption of this world and our bodies. They help us to remember (and rejoice) that this world is not our home, that we are sojourners, aliens.

Now, in one great sense, of course, this world is our home. But not as it is. One day God will remake it, and we will enjoy the new creation that is brimming with the glory of his Son and where pain and suffering find no purchase. Because of this, the pain and suffering on this side of Christ's return help us to cry, "Even so, come, Lord Jesus!"—living expectantly and with a homesickness for heaven.

6. *To make us more like Christ, the suffering servant.* This appears to be God's chief use of suffering for the believer. It is never a punishment, since God has placed that on Christ at the cross. But it is always a disciplining, because in suffering God places Christ's cross in us.

In the context of Paul's words in Romans 8 on suffering, he writes, "For those whom he foreknew he also predestined to be conformed to the image of his Son" (Rom. 8:29). This is what Paul means when he says God is causing all things to work together for the good. We often take him to mean that all the bad things are going to give way into a world of good things—and that sometimes occurs—but what he really means is that all the bad things are culminating in us toward Christlikeness. To suffer, in the New Testament economy, is to "share abundantly in Christ's sufferings" (2 Cor. 1:5).

This is why Paul and the other apostles rejoiced in their suffering—because they thought being made to be like Jesus was the best thing that could happen to them. "For we who live are always being given over to death for Jesus' sake, so that the life of Jesus also may be manifested in our mortal flesh," Paul says (2 Cor. 4:11). There is more on that later in this chapter. But for now we may respond to the "why?" question with another question on God's behalf: "Why do we reckon ourselves better than Jesus?"

If suffering was good enough for him, shouldn't it be good enough for us?

In any event, the New Testament writers look at suffering as God's primary means of aligning us with the image of Christ. If we will be like him in his suffering, then we may be like him in his glory. Thomas Watson tells us, "Afflictions work for good, as they conform us to Christ. God's rod is a pencil to draw Christ's image more lively upon us."[2]

7. *To awaken the lost to their need for God.* God allows suffering so that people will see the brokenness of the world, despair of their ability to escape or conquer it themselves, and cry out to him for divine rescue. Or, as C. S. Lewis put it:

> We can rest contentedly in our sins and in our stupidities; and anyone who has watched gluttons shovelling down the most exquisite foods as if they did not know what they were eating, will admit that we can ignore even pleasure. But pain insists upon being attended to. God whispers to us in our pleasures, speaks in our conscience, but shouts in our pains: it is His megaphone to rouse a deaf world.[3]

We get a sense of this in Psalm 119, as David writes, "Before I was afflicted I went astray, but now I keep your word" (v. 67) and, "It is good for me that I was afflicted, that I might learn your statutes" (v. 71).

8. *To make the bliss of heaven more sweet.* Here is an interesting consideration: "For I consider that the sufferings of this present time are not worth comparing with the glory that is to be revealed to us" (Rom. 8:18).

Perhaps one way God makes heaven the all-consuming bliss it will be is by allowing the depths of all-touching suffering here. Should any of us have an "easy life," the wonders of heaven would still by contrast make this wondrous earth appear a pigsty. But given the pain we experience on this side of the parousia, the glory of the other side will be that much sweeter. "But rejoice insofar as you share Christ's sufferings, that you may also rejoice and be glad when his glory is revealed" (1 Pet. 4:13).

Indeed, as the Bible speaks of crowns and heavenly rewards, as the martyrs in Revelation are given the reward of their suffering, we are perhaps not far off the mark to suspect that those in Christ who suffer more in this life will enjoy him more greatly in

---

[2] Thomas Watson, *A Divine Cordial: Romans 8:28* (Lafayette, Indiana: Sovereign Grace, 2001), 21.
[3] C. S. Lewis, *The Business of Heaven: Daily Readings with C. S. Lewis* (Orlando, FL: Harcourt, 1984), 242.

the next. The great hymn writer Fanny Crosby appeared to think along these lines.

> "I think it is a great pity that the Master did not give you sight when he showered so many other gifts upon you," remarked one well-meaning preacher. Fanny Crosby responded at once, as she had heard such comments before. "Do you know that if at birth I had been able to make one petition, it would have been that I was born blind?" said the poet, who had been able to see only for her first six weeks of life. "Because when I get to heaven, the first face that shall ever gladden my sight will be that of my Savior."[4]

Lewis again:

> [Some mortals] say of some temporal suffering, "No future bliss can make up for it," not knowing that Heaven, once attained, will work backwards and turn even that agony into a glory.[5]

"Those who sow in tears shall reap with shouts of joy!" the psalmist tells us (Ps. 126:5). He will trade our ashes for beauty (Isa. 61:3). It is only logical to think "more ashes, more beauty."

9. *So that Christ will get the glory in being our strength.* We are allowed frailty so that Christ's strength would be magnified. This is what Jesus intimates when he says the man was born blind so "that the works of God might be displayed in him" (John 9:3). And it is exactly what Paul has in mind in 2 Corinthians 4:7: "But we have this treasure in jars of clay, to show that the surpassing power belongs to God and not to us."

Here we are, fragile and frail. But inside? The unassailable kingdom. The unstealable treasure of Christ. The unsurpassable glory of grace. In suffering, we are broken open. Then can be seen what we're made of.

10. *And so that, thereby, others see that he is our treasure, and not ourselves.* When these jars are broken, like cheap terra-cotta piggy banks, what's inside is revealed to any lookers-on. Suffering tests

---

[4] "Fanny Crosby," *Christian History Online*, August 8, 2008, http://www.christianitytoday.com/ch/131christians/poets/crosby.html?start=1.
[5] C. S. Lewis, *The Great Divorce* (New York: HarperCollins, 2001), 69.

(and conquers) our mettle. When we are trusting in Christ, we reveal that he is our strength, and we reveal that he is our treasure. *If* we have placed our faith in him. *If* we hurt authentically but also trust authentically. *If* we grieve as those who have hope (1 Thess. 4:13). If those conditions are present, our brokenness will reveal what our heart has laid hold of.

If these jars of clay hold the treasure of Christ, "we are afflicted in every way, but not crushed; perplexed, but not driven to despair; persecuted, but not forsaken; struck down, but not destroyed" (2 Cor. 4:8–9).

SUFFERING AND GOD'S GLORY

In the Scriptures we find that suffering and glory are inextricably linked. We have seen a few examples already. Here are a few more:

Was it not necessary that the Christ should suffer these things and enter into his glory? (Luke 24:26)

So I ask you not to lose heart over what I am suffering for you, which is your glory. (Eph. 3:13)

But we see him who for a little while was made lower than the angels, namely Jesus, crowned with glory and honor because of the suffering of death, so that by the grace of God he might taste death for everyone. For it was fitting that he, for whom and by whom all things exist, in bringing many sons to glory, should make the founder of their salvation perfect through suffering. (Heb. 2:9–10)

So I exhort the elders among you, as a fellow elder and a witness of the sufferings of Christ, as well as a partaker in the glory that is going to be revealed. (1 Pet. 5:1)

And after you have suffered a little while, the God of all grace, who has called you to his eternal glory in Christ, will himself restore, confirm, strengthen, and establish you. (1 Pet. 5:10)

As we have seen, God deigns to provide answers to the *why* question of suffering, but his Word is mainly interested in demonstrating that suffering is meant for his glory—and ours. This too is gospel. Because if sharing Christ's suffering is the way to share in his glory (2 Cor. 1:5; Phil. 3:10; 1 Pet. 4:13), and if the discipline of hardship is proof of God's treating us like a loving Father (Heb. 12:5–7), suffering as trusters of Jesus is *good*. This is why Paul and the apostles and the New Testament church rejoiced in their sufferings. They viewed suffering completely differently than we often do, and certainly differently than unbelievers always have. In the light of Christ, and in the knowledge of the glory of his cross (and resurrection), they viewed suffering as God's refining work in their lives, his training them to hope in the imperishable inheritance, and his fashioning them into a reflection of the Christ inside of them.

So it is that through the gospel's depths we see the true depths of suffering. The living Word redirects our gaze from self—which instinctively demands justification, asking, "Why?"—to the glorious God of all comfort. The gospel question to suffering is not *why* Jud Wilhite's words are helpful:

> The testimonies of the Bible about pain and suffering and the consequences of sin are not mathematical formulas for rational understanding. Instead they are constant proclamations about the God who rules and loves, and they are constant reminders to cast our cares upon him. God wants us to hope in *him*.
>
> In other words, *why* is not the most fundamental human question when it comes to suffering. Even if we had all the answers to our whys, we might actually find them unsatisfying and ultimately unredemptive for the pain we are facing. A bigger question emerges.
>
> The most fundamental question, according to the Bible, is *who*. Who will we trust in the calamities and challenges of life? Who will we turn to in the reality of our pain? *Who is worthy of our trust?*[6]

Precisely. We have offered a list of ten answers the Bible provides to *why* but even knowing them, and even if we had access to

---

[6]Jud Wilhite, *Torn: Trusting God When Life Leaves You in Pieces* (Colorado Springs: Multnomah, 2011), 6–7.

that inner-mind knowledge of God's sovereign motive, they would not remove the source of the question! As Rich Mullins sang, on his last album before his untimely death, "I know it would not hurt any less even if it could be explained."[7]

Instead of satisfying the logic of suffering to our heart's desire, God opts to satisfy the heart's desire that suffering brings to the surface. "And after you have suffered a little while, the God of all grace, who has called you to his eternal glory in Christ, will himself restore, confirm, strengthen, and establish you" (1 Pet. 5:10).

The New Testament writers in fact see suffering as itself a gift of grace. "Count it all joy, my brothers, when you meet trials of various kinds," James says, "for you know that the testing of your faith produces steadfastness" (James 1:2–3).

Paul, in fact, envisions suffering as something God allows us to have, as if we have qualified for it, as if it is a privilege! "For it has been granted to you," he writes, "that for the sake of Christ you should not only believe in him but also suffer for his sake" (Phil. 1:29). In 2 Corinthians 11, he catalogs the accumulated persecutions, tortures, illnesses, and other assorted hardships he has suffered. In the next chapter, he speaks of his "thorn in the flesh" (2 Cor. 12:7), which God has allowed him to suffer, against Paul's pleadings. In the end, Paul decides that God has gifted him suffering in order that he might know the fullest measure of grace possible.

> But he said to me, "My grace is sufficient for you, for my power is made perfect in weakness." Therefore I will boast all the more gladly of my weaknesses, so that the power of Christ may rest upon me. For the sake of Christ, then, I am content with weaknesses, insults, hardships, persecutions, and calamities. For when I am weak, then I am strong. (2 Cor. 12:9–10)

If we were strong and did not suffer, the glory would be ours. It would be our attributes that carry an eternal weight. Who does Superman glorify, after all, but himself? And so God has stuffed kryptonite into a hidden compartment in every superperson, ensuring that we will all without exception be in need of rescue

---

[7]Rich Mullins, "Hard to Get," *The Jesus Record* (Word Music, 1997).

and will groan until it takes place. In this way God is glorified and we are promised strength in our weakness.

Of course, we can take this too far. God may be calling us to martyrdom, but he is not calling us to a martyr's *complex*. The gift of glory through suffering is not about becoming gluttons for punishment. It is simply about finding the ability to rejoice not just after suffering, but *in* it, because of the way God purposes it to bring about the glory of himself and the presence of Christ in and through us.

As Christ suffered to conquer sin and the flesh, we suffer to slough off all vestiges of the perishable. We are being refined, sanctified. Suffering produces holiness for those who trust Jesus in it.

> So we do not lose heart. Though our outer self is wasting away, our inner self is being renewed day by day. For this light momentary affliction is preparing for us an eternal weight of glory beyond all comparison, as we look not to the things that are seen but to the things that are unseen. For the things that are seen are transient, but the things that are unseen are eternal. (2 Cor. 4:16–18)

There is glory for those who suffer in Christ Jesus. There is God's glory made manifest in our weakness, and there is the "eternal weight of glory beyond all comparison" that our suffering is paying into. We were built for glory and, indeed, right at this very moment we are hidden with Christ in his glory (Col. 3:3). As our bodies wind down, our glorification is winding up, preparing our soul for that great day of consummation, where every tear will be wiped away, where everything sad will become untrue, where the curse and its various degenerations will be seen as but a "light momentary affliction." Only the glory of God can accomplish such a thing, and what a gospel that in Christ he shares that with us!

CARRYING CHRIST'S DEATH AND MANIFESTING CHRIST'S LIFE IN OUR BODIES

Jesus is the radiance of the glory of God (Heb. 1:3). This means that all that is truly wondrous emanates from and converges in him. He is the intersection of infinite excellencies.

From the ungospeled perspective, however, suffering and goodness run infinitely parallel tracks. But the incarnation throws a wrench into this finite historical vision. Here comes the God-man, Jesus the Christ. He is fully God but fully man, tempted as we are, yet without sin (Heb. 4:15). The parallel lines begin to bend.

Jesus is able to sympathize with our weaknesses. He grows in wisdom and stature. He who is equal to the Father refuses to exploit his deity, submitting to the Father and becoming obedient even to the point of death. The parallel lines make a break, diving into each other, as if electromagnetically charged.

He who knew no sin became sin for us that we might become the righteousness of God (2 Cor. 5:21). The parallel tracks collide.

Suffering and God's goodness intersect at the cross.

Because of the collision of God's justice—in the setting to rights of all that is broken and the judgment of wrath poured out for disobedience—and God's mercy—in the substitution of his Son for the deserving enemies he loves, the cross is a thermonuclear explosion of saving ironies. In dying, he kills sin. In captivity, he is victorious. In exposure, he is exalted. In this end is the beginning.

The fallout is far-reaching. "He comes to make his blessings flow, far as the curse is found."[8] The power of the cross implants an inscrutable saving irony in us:

> I have been crucified with Christ. It is no longer I who live, but Christ who lives in me. And the life I now live in the flesh I live by faith in the Son of God, who loved me and gave himself for me. (Gal. 2:20)

I'm dead, but because I'm dead in Christ, I'm actually alive, because Christ is alive. "Now if we have died with Christ, we believe that we will also live with him" (Rom. 6:8). Through the power of the cross, we have found our lives by losing them (Matt. 16:25). Through the power of the cross, we are sculpted into a reflection of Christ's glory through our sharing in his crucifixion. Paul puts his crosshairs on this crosswise effect in 2 Corinthians 4:6–12:

---

[8] Isaac Watts, "Joy to the World," (1719).

For God, who said, "Let light shine out of darkness," has shone in our hearts to give the light of the knowledge of the glory of God in the face of Jesus Christ. But we have this treasure in jars of clay, to show that the surpassing power belongs to God and not to us. We are afflicted in every way, but not crushed; perplexed, but not driven to despair; persecuted, but not forsaken; struck down, but not destroyed; *always carrying in the body the death of Jesus, so that the life of Jesus may also be manifested in our bodies.* For we who live are always being given over to death for Jesus' sake, so that the life of Jesus also may be manifested in our mortal flesh. So death is at work in us, but life in you.

This is a beautiful, confounding passage. The image at work, again, is the frailty of a clay vessel concealing a priceless treasure ("the light of the knowledge of the glory of God in the face of Jesus Christ"). The purpose of suffering for the believer, then, is to reveal this light of Christ, to reveal the image of Christ, and we do this first by suffering as he suffered, by being conformed to the image of the crucified Savior. But how do we do that? How can we actively engage, in the midst of our hurts and brokenness, in carrying the death of Jesus in our bodies so that the life of Jesus is visible in our bodies?

We may look to the actual dying of Jesus for help. In four of his statements from the cross, we see the means of dying and dying to ourselves in a cross-centered way.

HONESTY WITH GOD

"My God, my God, why have you forsaken me?" our Savior cries (Matt. 27:46).

Jesus is quoting Psalm 22, which is ultimately about *not* being forsaken by God—but the opening of the psalm and Jesus's words here are certainly about the relational rift between the Father and himself. Calvin writes:

No one who considers that Christ undertook the office of Mediator on the condition of suffering our condemnation, both in his body and in his soul, will think it strange that he maintained a struggle with the sorrows of death, as if an offended God had thrown him into a whirlpool of afflictions.[9]

In this we find the okay to be honest with God. Many times, either out of fear of the pain of further vulnerability or out of bad theology that tells us to put on a happy face or God won't like us, we hold back from God, thinking we may leverage his healing or his comfort or his approval by sucking it up and pretending we aren't hurting. But the psalmists don't do this. The prophets don't do this. And Jesus didn't do this. You can't hide anything from God anyway. He sees you're hurting. Be honest with him. He can take it. Being honest with God is the way of holding no part of ourselves back, the way of laying it all on the altar for his dealing. This is precisely what Jesus did, even in his anguish. We show that Jesus was *real*, accessing his glory in more ways than one and receiving his gospel, when we agree to expose all to God.

FORGIVENESS

As his captors mock, torture, and execute him, Jesus prays, "Father, forgive them, for they know not what they do" (Luke 23:34).

One ironic way to embrace the power of God in the midst of hurt is to forgive those who have hurt you. Unforgiveness brews bitterness, which does not alleviate pain but exacerbates it. When we forgive our enemies and bless those who persecute us, we glorify God by acknowledging that he is the sovereign Judge over all and that vengeance is his. And we highlight the treasure of Christ, who forgave all the way to death those who hate him.

Forgiveness requires the death even of our egos, the suffering of our pride. Therefore, as we suffer, even unjustly, we may manifest the life-giving grace of Jesus Christ as we embody the life-taking sacrifice of Jesus Christ. A forgiving sufferer makes Jesus look *big*.

SUBMISSION TO GOD'S SOVEREIGNTY

On the verge of his last breath, Jesus exclaims, "Father, into your hands I commit my spirit!" (Luke 23:46).

---

[9]John Calvin, *Commentary on Matthew*, Christian Classics Ethereal Library, http://www.ccel.org/ccel/calvin/calcom33.ii.xlii.html.

This is the dying man's way of saying, "Not my will, but yours, be done" (Luke 22:42). Every Christian can see suffering as a gift from God, but every honest sufferer prefers comfort to suffering. God may seem to delay. There may be no end to suffering in sight. As Christians, what we can know is that God has purposed pain to remind us that the world and those of us who live in it are broken, fallen because of sin. We can know, thanks to the revelation of God that is his written Word, that the grand purpose of suffering for the Christian is to be conformed to the image of Christ. We can commit our spirit into the Father's hands by ditching our pleas for fairness and trusting that God is revealing the treasure of Christ in our bodies through our bodies' very decay.

Let us look forward to the resurrection, when we will have new, imperishable bodies, powered by the Spirit and awash in the glory of the risen Son (1 Cor. 15:42–49). Let us amen Job's oath: "Though he slay me, I will hope in him" (Job 13:15). The sufferer who is able to submit in faith to God's sovereignty this way manifests Christ's life in his suffering, for Christ was totally submitted to the will of the Father in his cross-taking mission.

CENTEREDNESS ON THE GOSPEL

In his despair, Jesus has already echoed Psalm 22's opening line. In his victory, then, he echoes Psalm 22's closing line ("he has done it," v. 31), declaring, "It is finished" (John 19:30).

The work is done. This is the great message of the good news: he has done it! We can hope in our suffering, then, that the finished work of Christ, when believed with our hearts, is the catalyst to the refining work begun in us. The gospel tells us that we are forgiven from sin, that we stand under grace, that we have the blessed hope of Christ's return, that we will be resurrected as he was, and that we stand to receive the inheritance of Christ's rich presence in the new heavens and the new earth.

The gospel tells us that God will be faithful to finish the work he started. So the fragility of our jars of clay is not just our preparing for the grave, but our equipping for eternity. When we center on the gospel as we suffer, we communicate as dying men to dying men that there is real hope for real people. We make Christ manifest in this witness. With Job we can declare, "And after my skin has been thus destroyed, yet in my flesh I shall see God, whom I shall see for myself, and my eyes shall behold" (Job 19:26–27). And: "I know that my Redeemer lives, and at the last he will stand upon the earth" (Job 19:25).

If we can apply Jesus's words from the cross in our times of suffering, we can carry the cross-shaped death of Jesus in our bodies, thereby revealing that he who is the life everlasting is our true treasure.

PHILIPPIANS AND THE SUFFERING DESCENT TO GLORY

We can know suffering as glory if we will know the glory of the cross.

This will involve the stooping, the feeling of the weight on our backs, the taunts, the reaching the end of ourselves. The book of Philippians is a staircase of sorts, down into the depths of loss, wherein is great gain. Philippians charts the gospel deeps.

The first chapter surveys Paul's giving up of his rights—to freedom in imprisonment, to self in Christ's eclipse of ministerial competition and resentment, to safety in his precarious situation, to control in his resignation to either life or death. "To live is Christ, and to die is gain" (Phil. 1:21). He has taken one giant step beneath the surface of the afflicted flesh.

In Philippians 2, he goes another step down, beneath the physical chains on his flesh, beneath the impending loss of his physical life. The state of the mind is greater in play. We will want Jesus, because he emptied himself and thereby came to exaltation. "Work out your own salvation with fear and trembling," then (2:12). Christ is at work in affliction on you, but he is at work in glory *in* you. Paul has given up selfish ambition, a harder buffeting to suffer, but the buffeting of his body has helped. He has descended deeper into the wounds of Christ, seeing his life as but a drink offering to be poured out for the church (2:17).

Another level down now, in Philippians 3, Paul has given up all confidence in the flesh. Despite all his accomplishments, he feels the death in his flesh, so he knows his flesh cannot be held onto. But he has felt the death inside too. He will not have his jar of clay filled up with moth-eaten, rusty badges of honor, which is not any better than emptiness.

> Indeed, I count everything as loss because of the surpassing worth of knowing Christ Jesus my Lord. For his sake I have suffered the loss of all things and count them as rubbish, in order that I may gain Christ and be found in him, not having a righteousness of my own that comes from the law, but that which comes through faith in Christ, the righteousness from God that depends on faith—that I may know him and the power of his resurrection, and may share his sufferings, becoming like him in his death, that by any means possible I may attain the resurrection from the dead. (3:8–11)

He is very near the bottom of himself now. His body is "lowly" (Phil. 3:21) and therefore ripe for glory. It is at this point that temptation to discontentment can be greatest. "Why have you forsaken me, God? I am at my lowest point. How can I be satisfied in any way with this?"

Philippians 4 finds Paul lower than lower—and higher than high!—as he forfeits in his suffering the response of dissatisfaction.

> The Lord is at hand; do not be anxious about anything, but in everything by prayer and supplication with thanksgiving let your requests be made known to God. And the peace of God, which surpasses all understanding, will guard your hearts and your minds in Christ Jesus. (4:5–7)

"I know how to be brought low," he says. "I have learned the secret" (4:12).

Yes, there he is, having gone all the way down, step by step, receiving the gospel further and further into himself, pushing deeper into the glory of suffering, where the crucified Savior holds out his wounded yet glorified arms. In the secret place Christ's death is life, so our weakness is strength. We can in fact do all things through him (4:13).

There is Paul, in his prison cell, having reached the end of himself, having descended the Via Dolorosa and found himself in the cellar of affliction, where God keeps the best wine.

Chapter Seven

AS FAR AS EAST
FROM WEST

"It seems, then," said Tirian, smiling himself,
"that the Stable seen from within and the stable
seen from without are two different places."
"Yes," said the Lord Digory. "Its inside is bigger
than its outside."—C. S. Lewis[1]

In T. S. Eliot's masterpiece of British modernism "The Waste Land,"
his sailor rides the river Thames, declared both "dull" and "sweet,"
as one searching among the ruins of civilization for some harmo-
nious semblance of bygone days.

> A current under sea
> Picked his bones in whispers. As he rose and fell
> He passed the stages of his age and youth
> Entering the whirlpool.[2]

He sails through the fractured world, seeking sense in what
Lewis calls "gleams of celestial strength and beauty falling on a
jungle of filth and imbecility."[3] Onward he forges, through oil and
tar, through the dim brown fog of London, haunted by echoes
of Christendom—those whispers picking at his bones in the current—reminiscent of "The horror! The horror!"[4] engulfing Conrad's
boatmen as they venture through the sepulchral city in *Heart of
Darkness*.

The apostle Peter calls these sailors "elect exiles of the Dis-

---

[1] C. S. Lewis, *The Last Battle* (New York: Macmillan, 1970), 140.
[2] T. S. Eliot, "The Waste Land," iv.4–7, in *"The Waste Land" and Other Poems* (Orlando, FL: Har-court Brace, 1962), 41.
[3] C. S. Lewis, *Perelandra* (New York: Macmillan, 1965), 201.
[4] Joseph Conrad, *Heart of Darkness*, in *Heart of Darkness and The Secret Sharer* (New York: Signet, 1997), 164.

person" (1 Pet. 1:1), and they are us. The world is a beautiful place, but broken. We enjoy it, but we are constantly haunted by Eden past. And by the New Jerusalem to come. As we explore the depths of the gospel, then, we are learning to cast ourselves into the great glorious unknown of God's upward tide. Eliot's sailor and Conrad's sailor are seeking the restoration we see in the increasing revelation of the good news of Jesus.

Having taken up our cross to follow him, we have pushed off from the shallows. Journeying ever onward, we are exploring the deep things of God. Call us Ishmael, for "Already we are boldly launched upon the deep; but soon we shall be lost in its unshored, harborless immensities."[5]

God's glory in the gospel cannot be circumnavigated. We are not exploring in that sense. There is no route to take but "further up and further in." To know God better is to know better that eternity won't exhaust his knowability.

But God is equipping us more and more to search out more and more of him. "I will run in the way of your commandments," David sings, "when you enlarge my heart!" (Ps. 119:32). Richard Sibbes echoes:

> Let us remember that grace is increased, in the exercise of it, not by virtue of the exercise itself, but as Christ by his Spirit flows into the soul and brings us nearer to himself, the fountain, so instilling such comfort that the heart is further enlarged.[6]

We will need this larger heart in order to have the "strength to comprehend with all the saints what is the breadth and length and height and depth" (Eph. 3:18). God fills us with the Spiritual energy to sail about on his infinite majesties, his harborless immensities.

What will we see in our travels? Those things from the deep that only haunt the Spiritless as whispers picking at the bones, mists, shadows, rumors of another world, fuzzy snapshots of cryptozoological specters. What has captured the imagination of all men as sense, myth, even fairy magic, firms up in its source, takes

---

[5] Herman Melville, *Moby Dick* (New York: Penguin, 2009), 145.
[6] Richard Sibbes, *The Bruised Reed* (Carlisle, PA: Banner of Truth Trust, 1998), 71.

shape, lives and breathes, but one must have the eyes to see, and these only the Spirit of the one true God gives.

But, as it is written,

> "What no eye has seen, nor ear heard,
>   nor the heart of man imagined,
> what God has prepared for those who love him"—

these things God has revealed to us through the Spirit. For the Spirit searches everything, even the depths of God. (1 Cor. 2:9–10)

We will see the real culmination of history, its ascended Redeemer and the legions of angels at his disposal. He will be the sun of the new creation (Rev. 21:23). What will the restored world look like in the light of the radiant Son? "There be many excellent things in Christ, that the most eagle-eyed believer hath not yet seen."[7]

Blissfully adrift in the gospel, you could not imagine in your mind the wonders you will actually see with your eyes!

God has been cooking this stuff up since before time began, in the bright shadows of eternity past.

THE GOSPEL'S LENGTH

Before anything was, God is. Perfectly self-sufficient, he has always existed. Father, Son, and Holy Spirit were perfect, needful of nothing, company from ever before. But in the timeless antecedent of eternity past, the plan of the gospel was already in effect. Before the earth was fashioned out of the void, before Adam and Eve were created, before the fall of mankind in Adam's sin, in the everlasting "before," the Father foreknew every one of his own and set his redemptive designs on them. From the fountain of God's foreknowledge in ageless past flows the eternal life for God's time-bound children.

The knowledge of Romans 8:29 is almost too wonderful: "For those whom he foreknew he also predestined to be conformed to

---

[7]John Flavel, *The Whole Works of the Rev. Mr. John Flavel* (London: W. Baynes and Son, 1820), 1:39.

the image of his Son." Not just centuries ago, not just eons ago, but before there were centuries or eons, or seconds or nanoseconds for that matter, God in his holy solitude *knew* us and predetermined that we would be won to Christ.

The gospel begins before there were any beginnings. And the Scriptures don't simply speak of this in terms of God's motivation or intention, but even in terms of actualization. Meaning, God's redemptive designs on us weren't limited just to his thinking, but expanded, before the world was created, to his doing. We see a glimpse of this in Revelation 13:8 and 17:8 where we learn that the names of the redeemed were written in the Lamb's book of life "before the foundation of the world." Matthew 25:34 tells us that the kingdom was prepared for us before the foundation of the world. Ephesians 1:4 says God chose us in Christ before the foundation of the world. Before the foundation of the world, the gospel is already unfolding. "But we impart a secret and hidden wisdom of God, which God decreed before the ages for our glory" (1 Cor. 2:7).

This deep knowledge ought to shatter the open theist's gospel-as-contingency-plan. He supposes there is no future for God to know; however, the Bible reveals that not only does God know the future before the future exists, but he is doing things *before* time that will take their effect *in* time. With Marty McFly we say, "Heavy."

In eternity past, the Son of God began his saving vocation—his "coming forth is from of old, from ancient days" (Mic. 5:2)—before there were any sins to forgive. The "hope of eternal life, which God, who never lies, promised before the ages began" (Titus 1:2), *began* before the ages began! Paul says to Timothy that God actually gave us the grace of Jesus before there was time (2 Tim. 1:9). His love is given to us ever always (Ps. 103:17). Reflecting on the ever-lasting precedence of the covenant of grace, in conjunction with Isaiah 54:5, John Gill reflects, "Christ is said to be the husband of the Gentile church before she was in actual being."[8]

We cannot measure the gospel's length because it is lengthless,

---

[8]John Gill, *A Body of Doctrinal Divinity* (Paris, AR: The Baptist Standard Bearer, 2001), 200.

beginning in the wisdom and doing of God from eternity past and stretching forth into eternity future. This is why life in Christ is called "everlasting."

THE GOSPEL OF THE DIVINE ATTRIBUTES

In 1 Timothy 1:3–11, Paul warns Timothy about false teachers, and as he surveys the weight of sin for which the law is suitable to reveal, he counterweights these specified rebellions with "sound doctrine, in accordance with the gospel of the glory of the blessed God with which I have been entrusted" (1 Tim. 3:10–11). It is a beautiful and deep turn of phrase. *The gospel of the glory of the blessed God.* Everything we learn about the gospel of Jesus's death, burial, and resurrection is summarily the news of God's glory.

What is glory? It is the revealed splendor of what something essentially is. As it pertains to YHWH God, glory is weightiness. God's glory is the sum of all God is, the gathered awesomeness of his attributes. This is a weight infinitely heavier than all the Bible's lists of sins!

So now we have Paul saying to Timothy that the gospel is in some sense "the glory of God." How so? For a few reasons, not the least of which is that the gospel declares the work of Jesus, who himself is the radiance of God's glory (Heb. 1:3), but also because the gospel is God-shaped in its working and because it seeds the world with what will result in the knowledge of the glory of God filling the earth like the waters cover the sea (Hab. 2:14).

The gospel is God's glory also because it brings God's attributes to bear for our salvation. One intriguing glimpse we get of this truth is found in Galatians 3:19–20, in which we see how what Arthur Pink calls the "solitariness of God" works to effect our reconciliation to him as Father.[9] As Paul educates us in the function of the Mosaic Law, he relates how God's self-sufficiency works to our benefit and community:

> Why then the law? It was added because of transgressions, until
> the offspring should come to whom the promise had been made,

---

[9] Arthur W. Pink, *The Attributes of God* (Grand Rapids, MI: Baker, 2006), 9–14.

and it was put in place through angels by an intermediary. Now an intermediary implies more than one, but God is one. (Gal. 3:19–20)

As I prepared to preach once on Galatians 3:15–22, those two verses gave me the biggest headache. I could get a tentative handle on verse 19. But verse 20's conciseness belied the frustration therein. Galatians 3:20 is like Manny Pacquiao: it doesn't look like much, but it will tear you up. At least, it did me.

I chewed on it and chewed on it. I looked at it from different angles. I stared at it like it was one of those optical illusion pictures they sell at the mall. Didn't work. The commentaries I consulted weren't much help. Luther had been my homeboy throughout my journey through Galatians, and his commentary is otherwise a masterpiece, but his comment on this text only seemed to extrapolate further on verse 19. I wanted to know what God being "one" had to do with intermediaries involved in dispensing the Law. It seemed like the answer should be obvious. I felt like a dog who'd just been handed a Rubik's cube.

The editor's note in Calvin's commentary said that another commentator estimated that there were 250 possible interpretations of Galatians 3:20. This was both comforting and deflating. One commentary I pulled from the shelf skipped over verse 20 as if it didn't even exist. The exposition goes straight from 3:19 to 3:21. (As if we wouldn't notice.)

I had run up against the deeps of the gospel in this one verse—it's bigger inside than outside, remember!—and found myself overwhelmed, but beautifully frustrated.

Do you know those little pill-looking sponge things you can get at the dollar store for the kids? You put them in a glass of water and the plastic capsule dissolves or gives way over time and the wadded sponge expands and it turns out to be a duckie or a dinosaur or whatever? That's how (I think) I eventually experienced the awesomeness in Galatians 3:20. I just let it steep. Slowly its pill expanded in my mind.

Here's what I think it means (and I figure I have at least a 1 in 250 shot at being right): The Law was put in place via angels, through Moses. We see this affirmed in Acts 7:38 and 53 and in Hebrews 2:2. Deuteronomy 33:2 tells us it came to Sinai by "ten thousands of holy ones." That's a pretty impressive scene. "An intermediary implies more than one," Paul says. There were several links in the chain of command: from God via his ten thousand holy ones to Moses, then to the people. And let's not forget to factor in the priests and the ceremonial rites and regulations that went along with all that. In order to deliver—and then to administer—the Law, teamwork, as they say, made the dream work.

"But God is one."

Why is the gospel better than the Law? Why is Jesus more glorious than any other intermediary? Because it is God himself doing the job himself for the people *all by himself.* Consider the exhaustive and exhausting comprehensiveness and rigor that the Law entails. Multiply that by the glory that radiated on Moses's face, that was transmitted on a mountaintop via ten thousand flaming angels. Multiply that by precise measurements, a routine cycle of sacrifices, and an every-T-crossed attention to detail. Now consider that Christ Jesus is more glorious, more precise, more fulfilling, more encompassing than all that. And then! Consider that Jesus doesn't just hold up his end of the covenant of righteousness: he holds up our end too. An intermediary implies more than one. But God is one. He does his job, *and ours.*

That's what I think Galatians 3:20 means. I believe that is in keeping with the trajectory of the passage and the context of the book of Galatians itself, which is to say that the Law is good (for what it's designed to do), but that Jesus is much, much better. The Law is awesome, but the gospel is awesomer than awesome. Elsewhere Paul writes:

> Now if the ministry of death, carved in letters on stone, came with such glory that the Israelites could not gaze at Moses' face because of its glory, which was being brought to an end, will not the ministry of the Spirit have even more glory? For if there was glory in the ministry of condemnation, the ministry of righteousness must far exceed it in glory. Indeed, in this case, what

once had glory has come to have no glory at all, because of the glory that surpasses it. (2 Cor. 3:7–10)

Here we see how the gospel is God's glory because it brings to us the benefit of his self-sufficiency; it proclaims how our God, who needs nothing, saves the needy. It is a benefit to us because God does all by himself what we could not do even with the help of the Law and because it gives us the joy of knowing that our perfect God employed his perfection for his imperfect creatures.

We see throughout the Scriptures how the gospel brings to bear others of God's attributes as well.

As the gospel begins in the mind of God from eternity past, and as it encompasses every infinite contingency and permutation of history future, sovereignly directing the steps of men who plan their courses (Prov. 16:9), working in accordance with prophetic prescience (1 Cor. 15:3–4), flowing from the fountain of God's fore-knowledge (1 Pet. 1:2), it is not difficult to see how the gospel is the glory of the omniscient God.

The gospel brings God's omniscience to bear because nobody can forgive a sin of which he is unaware, yet God forgives us in Christ at the cross once for all time. Therefore, he must see not just our past sins and our secret sins, but he must see our tomorrow and next-year sins and all the rest.

It is easy to see God's omnipotence at work in the gospel. To undo the curse as far as it is found, to defeat the powers of sin and Satan, to forgive sins, to redeem the captives, to heal the sick, to restore the fortunes of the poor, to clothe the naked, to resurrect the dead, to renew and restore creation, and to sustain the whole lot of it all requires a level of power that is all-encompassing. Hebrews 1:3 says that Christ upholds the universe just by "the word of his power." The power to create *ex nihilo* what we see and what we (except for God himself) don't see must come from an "all-power." The power to re-create all that is created must come from an "all-power." The triune God is this all-power, and the gospel's earth-shattering and earth-renewing power emanates from his infinite might.

One of the more mindboggling meditations available, however, is on the gospel blessing of God's omnipresence.

CHRIST INCARNATE AND OMNIPRESENT

Once after I had preached on the ascension of Christ's glorified body to the right hand of the Father, extolling the wonders of that heavenly space, which is invisible and spiritual yet inhabited by physical and material presence, and holding up the vision of the day that that space fully becomes this space, a fellow came up to me and said, "Isn't it neat that Jesus loves us so much he has committed to eternal incarnation to the point of giving up his omnipresence forever?"

In my post-sermon shell shock, I just sort of nodded and said, "Yes, I guess so." I must repent, because I know it's not only not neat—it's not true. Jesus has not given up his omnipresence. Despite his eternal inhabitancy of a glorified body, he is still enjoying in some incomprehensible way his omnipresence.

Jesus is most definitely *there*. But he is also *here*.

And he always has been both here and there, even when he was incarnate on the earth. Together let's behold this inscrutable reality.

Philippians 2 shows us a great wonder; namely, the self-emptying of the Son of God.

> Let each of you look not only to his own interests, but also to the interests of others. Have this mind among yourselves, which is yours in Christ Jesus, who, though he was in the form of God, did not count equality with God a thing to be grasped, but emptied himself, taking the form of a servant, being born in the likeness of men. (Phil. 2:4–7)

Never has "nothingness" been so deep. Many scholars believe these lines come from an early hymn, and if this is true, we see in the form of the thing how Jesus Christ's willful, sacrificial self-emptying provokes worshipful response. But we also see in the *content* of the thing how Christ's condescending work provokes worshipful response. It cannot be grasped that he counted his equality with God not to be grasped. It is a truth filling to overflowing that he emptied himself ("made himself nothing" in the NIV; "stripped Himself of His glory" in Weymouth). The New Testament worshipers might have sung this early hymn because it is so bewilderingly wonderful that you have to. That we might put Christ's emptying of himself into our exaltation of him is an appropriate artistic representation of the upside-down way Jesus sets things to rights.

But we can go too far in our understanding of the *kenosis* of Philippians 2. Jesus gave up the option to exploit his deity; he self-limited employment of his attributes. But he did not *lose* them. He did not cease to be God, nor did he cease access to his 100 percent God-ness. As Phil Johnson says, "The incarnation was a miracle of addition, not subtraction."[10]

The incarnate Word of God, tempted and tried, was and is still the omnipresent God. Take a breath. Boggle.

Okay? Let's resume.

"Jesus said to them, 'Truly, truly, I say to you, before Abraham was, I am'" (John 8:58). This is not just an appropriation of the divine name (YHWH, "I AM"); it is an *assertion* of it. This is underneath the text: "This human being speaking to you right now is the everlasting God, the same God as the God of your fathers." This is on top of the text: "The place in time before your father Abraham was, I currently am." God incarnate in Jesus the Christ is, in some ineffable sense that the Bible barely approaches out of compensation for our feeble minds, simultaneously outside of time. He was there talking to the Jewish leaders, and at the same time there before they were born. He is not just saying he existed before Abraham, although that is true. He is not just saying he is superior to Abraham, though he is saying that. He is saying that because he is fully God, he is currently in time and out of it.

There is more.

"And no man hath ascended up to heaven, but he that came down from heaven, even the Son of man which is in heaven" (John 3:13 KJV). The ESV translates this verse, "No one has ascended into

---

[10] Phil Johnson, "Kenosis and the Omnipresence of Christ," *Pyromaniacs* (blog), August 25, 2011, http://teampyro.blogspot.com/2011/08/kenosis-and-omnipresence-of-christ.html.

heaven except he who descended from heaven, the Son of Man," noting the variant text of "who is in heaven" in a footnote. Both Ridderbos and Carson note that this verse is difficult to translate and exegete.[11] Is Jesus saying that he is *from* heaven, or that he is *in* heaven? David Alan Black argues for the inclusion of the variant "who is in heaven" manuscript text fairly compellingly.[12] Our argument does not hinge on this one verse, but we have good reasons to pin a portion of it here. As Black notes, we do not see clear reasons why this phrase would be added as a later theological gloss, when what it seeks to add is already present elsewhere in John's Gospel. And the reasons for supposing its later addition would be the same for supposing its originality—it matches John's christology. Black elaborates, connecting the text to, as examples, John 1:14 and 51:

> The Johannine Jesus is not only the preexistent Word (1:1) and the post-resurrection exalted Christ (20:28), but also the Revealer and Savior who remained "with God" while present in the "flesh" (1:1, 14). The apparent anomaly of having God explain God (cf. 1:18) is reconciled in John's doctrine of the incarnate Logos. In the person of Jesus Christ, heaven has come to earth and earth has been linked with heaven. The Word which became flesh did not cease to be what he was before, for the flesh assumed by the Logos at the incarnation was the "tabernacle" (to use John's expression in 1:14) in which God was pleased to dwell with men. Thus the witness who apprehended the divinity of the eternal Logos in and in spite of the flesh could testify, "And we beheld his glory, the glory as of the only-begotten of the Father, full of grace and truth" (1:14). One could also point in this connection to 1:51, where the expression "Son of Man" is first used in John: "You shall see the heaven opened, and the angels of God ascending and descending upon the Son of Man." . . . In 3:13 John is giving expression, in a similarly dramatic way, to the consciousness of Jesus, who himself "ascends" and "descends."[13]

---

[11] See Herman Ridderbos, *The Gospel of John: A Theological Commentary*, trans. John Vriend (Grand Rapids, MI: Eerdmans, 1992), 134–36; and D. A. Carson, *The Gospel According to John*, Pillar Commentary Series (Grand Rapids, MI: Eerdmans, 1991), 199–201.

[12] David Alan Black, "The Text of John 3:13," *The Grace Theological Journal*, 6.1 (1985): 49–66, http://faculty.gordon.edu/hu/bi/Ted_Hildebrandt/NTeSources/NTArticles/GTJ-NT/Black-Jn3-GTJ-85.pdf.

[13] Ibid., 58–59.

Whatever we make of John 3:13, long or short, the thrust of Christ as the incarnate Logos opening, as it were, heaven to earth conveys the goodness of his eternal omnipresence. As Black has intimated, one elegant solution to the problem of the simultaneous incarnation and omnipresence of Jesus Christ is not just noting, as Phil Johnson says, that the incarnation is a miracle of addition, but also revisiting our conception of heaven itself. If it is not, strictly speaking, a time-bound locale taking up physical space, but somehow hyperdimensional and hyperspatial, outside of time and over time, we can make out the concept of heaven as essentially the place where God is. And if heaven is the place where God is, we may jettison the notion of heaven as a land in outer space and adopt a view of it as bigger than outer space yet residing somehow in inner space. "The kingdom of heaven is at hand," the Lord and his disciples declared (Matt. 3:2; 4:17; 10:7). Heaven is not just Matthew's circumlocution of the divine name; it is here and elsewhere the name for God's manifest presence and irresistible reign. In the Gospels we see that heaven is somehow coming to earth in and through the work of the Messiah Jesus. Heaven is the place where God is, the place where only his will is done. It is through the Bible's revelation of Christ's redemptive work that we begin to see that someday that place will become this place.

John Calvin does not wrestle much with the evident paradox of John 3:13, but simply revels in it, writing:

> It may seem absurd to say that he "is in heaven" while he still lives on earth. If it is answered that this is true about his divine nature, then this expression would mean something else—namely, that while he was man he was "in heaven." I could point out that no place is mentioned here and that only Christ is distinguished from everybody else as far as his state is concerned, since he is the heir of the kingdom of God, from which the whole human race is banished. However, as very frequently happens, because of the unity of the person of Christ, what correctly applies to one of his natures is applied to another of his natures, and so we need seek no other solution. So Christ, who "is in heaven," has clothed

himself in our flesh, so that by stretching out his brotherly hand to us he may raise us to heaven with himself.[14]

As Calvin sees it, Christ's descent from heaven to incarnate human flesh was not his *exit* from heaven. Indeed, Jesus, while in the throes of human angst and pain, states that the Father is in him and he is in the Father (John 17:21), and surely he does not mean merely in an "of one mind" sense but in the sense of "one presence" (even as he and we maintain the Trinitarian distinction between persons). This makes sense when we define heaven in terms of God's omnipresence rather than defining his omnipresence by our spatial conception of heaven.

Millard Erickson writes of Jesus:

> He had possessed the capability of active omnipresence: being pure spirit, he was not limited to any particular place and time. But as part of the decision to become incarnate, he also decided not to exercise that capability, or to make it latent, for a period of time.[15]

I fear this narrows omnipresence to an activity, not an attribute. Certainly Jesus did not teleport himself to every location around the globe in his incarnate body, but in the same way that divine omnipotence may be ever present in Christ without his employment of its capabilities at all times, he may maintain the ever-present attribute of omnipresence without employing it in every specific way possible. In other words, omnipresence for the Son of God is not simply a tool on a utility belt. Erickson's treatment in my mind unreasonably connects Jesus's refusal to employ his omnipresence in his incarnate body with his inability to do so. Earlier, Erickson writes, "It was not that he was pretending that he could not use it; he really could not."[16] I think with this we should disagree. Again, to say that Jesus did not "grasp" his omnipresence is not to say he did not maintain it (Phil. 2:6). It is to say that he

---

[14] John Calvin, *John*, Crossway Classic Commentaries, ed. Alister McGrath and J. I. Packer (Wheaton, IL: Crossway, 1994), 74–75.
[15] Millard J. Erickson, *The Word Became Flesh: A Contemporary Incarnational Christology* (Grand Rapids, MI: Baker, 1991), 561.
[16] Ibid., 549.

did not exploit it. If Jesus could not use his omnipresence, then we may have affirmed his 100 percent humanity but we have denied his 100 percent divinity.

To deny the incarnate Christ's omnipresence, then, is to deny his deity, because God cannot *not* be omnipresent. Louis Berkhof is helpful here:

> The doctrine of creation and the doctrine of the incarnation always constituted a problem in connection with the immutability of God. . . . However this problem may be solved, it should be maintained that the divine nature did not undergo any essential change in the incarnation. This also means that it remained impassible, that is, incapable of suffering and death, free from ignorance, and insusceptible to weakness and temptation. . . . The result of the incarnation was that the divine Saviour could be ignorant and weak, could be tempted, and could suffer and die, not in His divine nature, but derivatively by virtue of His possession of a human nature.[17]

Calvin weighs in again:

> For even if the Word in his immeasurable essence united with the nature of man into one person, we do not imagine that he was confined therein. Here is something marvelous: the Son of God descended from heaven in such a way that, without leaving heaven, he willed to be borne in the virgin's womb, to go about the earth, and to hang upon the cross; yet he continuously filled the world even as he had done from the beginning![18]

Indeed, Hebrews 13:8 reminds us, "Jesus Christ is the same yesterday and today and forever." Jesus did not resume his omnipresence upon his resurrection or ascension, as if he had lost it at his Spiritual conception in Mary's womb. He continued his omnipresence.

And now that he is there, seated at the right hand of the Father (Luke 22:69; Eph. 1:20; Col. 3:1; Heb. 8:1), he is also still

---

[17] Louis Berkhof, *Systematic Theology* (Grand Rapids, MI: Eerdmans, 1996), 323–24.
[18] John Calvin, *Institutes of the Christian Religion*, ed. John T. McNeill, trans. Ford Lewis Battles, 2 vols. (Philadelphia: Westminster, 1960), 1:481.

here. Jesus himself says, "And behold, I am with you always, to the end of the age" (Matt. 28:20). Also: "For where two or three are gathered in my name, there am I among them" (Matt. 18:20). Paul says that Christ is in us (Col. 1:27). Christ says that he is in and with us:

> In that day you will know that I am in my Father, and you in me, and I in you. Whoever has my commandments and keeps them, he it is who loves me. And he who loves me will be loved by my Father, and I will love him and manifest myself to him. . . . If anyone loves me, he will keep my word, and my Father will love him, and we will come to him and make our home with him. (John 14:20–21, 23)

Christ was once here and also there. Christ is now there and also here. How, though, does this idea relate to the gospel? How is Christ's omnipresence good news?

THE GOSPEL OF CHRIST'S OMNIPRESENCE

We see the notes of omnipresence in the eternal quality of Christ's historical work. As the God-man submits his mortal flesh to the crushing shame of crucifixion, giving up his spirit to the presence of the Father, the fabric of time rips open.

> And behold, the curtain of the temple was torn in two, from top to bottom. And the earth shook, and the rocks were split. The tombs also were opened. And many bodies of the saints who had fallen asleep were raised. (Matt. 27:51–52)

The who did what, now? Heavens, this is cosmic stuff!

The holy of holies is exposed now because Christ's sacrifice has terminated what was temporary and opened up what is eternal. His thirty-three-year-old body did this. With blood, sweat, and tears, he has brought eternal life eucatastrophically to earth. The place shudders. And the tombs give up the saints because he has offered up his dead body as the wrench in the gears that brings the reversal of death. He lives a short life and dies that we might die a short while and live.

Christ dispatched more work in those three hours He suffered, than ever was or will be done by all creatures until eternity. It was a good six days of work when the world was made, and He had a principal hand in that; neither has He been idle since. But that three hours' work on the cross was more than all the other. More will not be done in eternity than virtually was done in those three hours.

As they say that eternity is all time contracted into an instant, so all time, past and to come, was contracted into those few hours, as well as the merit of them. For He then made work for the Spirit, and indeed for all three persons, to eternity. He did that which the Spirit is writing out in grace and glory forever, and all that ever was or will be done toward the saints was then perfected: "He perfected for ever them that are sanctified, by that one offering" (Heb 10:12, 14).[19]

Christ's omnipresence, as well as his possession of the other divine attributes, is also good news in John 17:20 when he prays for those who will later believe in him. In those brief moments, it is possible that every Christian throughout all time leapt into the eternal consciousness of his prayerful mind, that he saw each of us individually and prayed for us. The future was perhaps contracted into that prayer.

He is with us there in that garden, redeeming us there in his intercession for us, just as in his obedience for us in the desert temptation, his sacrifice for us on the cross, and his resurrection for us out of the grave. He prays for us, trusts for us, obeys for us, dies for us, and rises for us, so that we will be able to pray in him, trust in him, obey in him, die in him, and rise in him. This is good news!

Christ's omnipresence takes another gospel turn as the Scriptures urge the co-inhabitation of Jesus and his disciples. A sampling:

Whoever feeds on my flesh and drinks my blood abides in me, and I in him. (John 6:56)

---

[19] Thomas Goodwin, *A Habitual Sight of Him: The Christ-Centered Piety of Thomas Goodwin*, ed. Joel Beeke and Mark Jones (Grand Rapids, MI: Reformation Heritage, 2009), 63–64.

Abide in me, and I in you. As the branch cannot bear fruit by itself, unless it abides in the vine, neither can you, unless you abide in me. I am the vine; you are the branches. Whoever abides in me and I in him, he it is that bears much fruit, for apart from me you can do nothing. (John 15:4–5)

I have been crucified with Christ. It is no longer I who live, but Christ who lives in me. And the life I now live in the flesh I live by faith in the Son of God, who loved me and gave himself for me. (Gal. 2:20)

Eternal life is said to consist of Christ's being in us and our being in him. Because he is both there and here, if we are in him, we are both here and there, as well. This spiritual reality is hinted at when Paul reveals that "our citizenship is in heaven" (Phil. 3:20) but it is clarified further in Ephesians 2:4–6:

But God, being rich in mercy, because of the great love with which he loved us, even when we were dead in our trespasses, made us alive together with Christ—by grace you have been saved—and raised us up with him and seated us with him in the heavenly places in Christ Jesus.

Did you catch that? We are seated with Christ in the heavenly places. Because of Christ's omnipresence, we who are saved in him are in some way present with him in his exaltation, a place of eternal security, a sort of firstfruits of "where I am you may be also" (John 14:3).

Marcus Rainsford speaks truth: "Really, thought becomes giddy, and our poor feeble minds weary, in contemplating truths like these, but they are resting places for faith."[20]

This is not just the gospel of Christ's omnipresence; it is more specifically the gospel of being clothed in Jesus. Like the lost son, like Eliot's sailor, we sail through the wasteland of this broken world in gaudy rags, surveying the cursed landscape for signs of restoration, for a sense of heaven on earth. We spend our money,

---

[20] Marcus Rainsford, *Our Lord Prays for His Own: Thoughts on John 17* (Grand Rapids, MI: Kregel, 1985), 160.

eat our food, drink our drink, thinking somewhere in this messy indulgence we will experience the eternal kind of life. We find ourselves in a pigsty. But at the end of ourselves we find the beginning of Christ's infinite goodness.

Penitent to the homestead we stumble, proffering legal restitution, the assumption of hired-hand status. Dad waves all that nonsense off, presents us a feast, and clothes us in his best robe, the pride of his wardrobe, the righteousness of Christ.

We are home, and homeward further we venture into the height, depth, length, and width of the measureless wonders of our gracious God. They stretch as far as east to west, as Jesus does. He is there on our behalf before the foundation of the world, he is here in our hearts now and reigning over his creation, he is seated there at the Father's side, and he is coming quickly. In his self-sufficiency he restores us, in his omniscience he knows us, in his omnipotence he rescues us, and in his omnipresence he secures us at all times in all places. Derek Thomas reflects:

> God's love, then, is wedded to sovereign power and sovereign will. We say, "Where there's a will, there's a way," and when the will in question is God's, the way is certain. God wills to save us, to bring us home, and nothing can stop Him.[21]

The gospel of Christ's omnipresence is merely the foreword to union with Christ. To that wonder, and related wonders, we turn in chapter 8.

---

[21] Derek W. H. Thomas, *How the Gospel Brings Us All the Way Home* (Lake Mary, FL: Reformation Trust, 2011), 131.

Chapter Eight

THE FOLD

"I thought with myself, how excellent a Being that was,
and how happy I should be, if I might enjoy that God,
and be rapt up to him in heaven, and be as it were
swallowed up in him forever!"—Jonathan Edwards[1]

We are stardust, the folkie tells us, golden. And we've got to get ourselves back to the garden. Only we can't. We know deep down we belong there somehow, but every journey we take seems a wild-goose chase, a "striving after wind."[2] The Teacher says God "has put eternity into man's heart, yet so that he cannot find out what God has done from the beginning to the end" (Eccles. 3:11). Call it the God-shaped hole or whatever you like, but the spiritual appetite exists in every one of us. Inside we carry the eternity deficit, which is why we are never not worshiping *something*.

We are wired for pilgrimage. But if we are not venturing secure in Christ upon the gospel deeps, we are simply adrift, lost at sea.

We do not know where it is we mean to be going, really, but we sense vaguely that it is a mysterious place that will feel familiar, like home, like Lucy Pevensie discovering that the strange garden was both new to her and utterly familiar.[3]

SEHNSUCHT, THE LONGING FOR THE FOLD

The German philosophers and poets called this eternity-shaped heartache *Sehnsucht* (ZEN-sookt), by which is meant a practically indescribable longing, craving, or yearning. Lewis describes *Sehnsucht* this way: "We cannot tell it because it is a desire for something that has never actually appeared in our experi-

[1] Jonathan Edwards, "Memoirs of President Edwards," in *The Works of President Edwards* (New York: Leavitt, Trow, and Co., 1844), 1:19.
[2] Ecclesiastes 1:14 and throughout the book.
[3] C. S. Lewis, *The Last Battle* (New York: Macmillan, 1970), 180.

ence. We cannot hide it because our experience is constantly suggesting it."[4]

When we broke ourselves with our sin, the image of God in us was fractured, and the sound of its breaking is like a signal from our hearts sent out to deepest space in search of reception. In my estimation Lewis writes of *Sehnsucht* best. But other artists capture it well: poets Whitman, Eliot, Auden; novelists Austen, Auster, James; painters Van Gogh and Hokusai; musicians from Rachmaninoff to Radiohead; and the Bible's King Solomon, if he be Ecclesiastes' *Qoheleth*. These artists capture in a variety of ways what cannot really be captured, the active ache inside of us, our collective groaning with creation (Rom. 8:23).

We all groan. But we deal with it in different ways. What are some of the ways we attempt to handle *Sehnsucht*?

1. *We drug it*. Perhaps the most common way we stifle this longing for God is by pouring false gods into it. "Every one of us is, even from his mother's womb, a master craftsman of idols," Calvin says.[5] From meth to porn, shopping to Facebook, the world does not lack for anesthetics. Most people commit to an endless cycle of temporarily satiating *Sehnsucht*. The cycle is endless, of course, because drugs wear off.

2. *We deny it*. This approach often goes hand in hand with idolatry, and is at its core self-idolatry, as plenty of people simply say they aren't broken, they aren't missing anything, they don't have that "inconsolable longing." They've got a happy family in a nice house with a two-car garage supported by a good job, and nothing bad has happened to them, and they just don't think they have cause to suspect they long for anything more. Of these people, John Kramp wisely reminds us, "You can be lost and not know it."[6] Let's not pretend every person apart from Christ *feels* lost without Christ. And this is probably the most dangerous position to be in, for the Devil loves for us to be happy apart from Christ.

---

[4] C. S. Lewis, "The Weight of Glory," in *"The Weight of Glory" and Other Addresses* (New York: HarperCollins, 2001), 30.
[5] From Calvin's *Commentary on the Acts of the Apostles*, cited in W. Robert Godfrey, *John Calvin: Pilgrim and Pastor* (Wheaton, IL: Crossway, 2001), 79.
[6] John Kramp, *Out of Their Faces and into Their Shoes* (Nashville: Broadman and Holman, 1995), 31.

3. *We deify it.* This approach is becoming more popular in professing Christian circles, particularly among younger generations. At some point, the longing itself becomes more interesting than the longed-for. Idolaters of *Sehnsucht* don't mind reveling in the mysteries at the expense of their Author, because mystery seems so much more interesting than revelation. Those who settle for the longing itself rather than the settler of the longing coddle their doubts, cherish subjectivity, and elevate uncertainty.

4. *We delight it.* "If you knew the gift of God, and who it is that is saying to you, 'Give me a drink,'" Jesus says to the woman, "you would have asked him, and he would have given you living water" (John 4:10).

How do you delight the longing? By finding the receiver tuned to its frequency. Only the enjoyment of God himself makes *Sehnsucht* truly beautiful. Only the rest of the Savior finally resolves our weariness. The cry of our hearts has one authorized interpreter, and this once unknown tongue, this one-time lament, this once barbarous yawp (thank you, Whitman), translates to a *joyous* yawp when spoken in its native land.

"Thou hast formed us for Thyself, and our hearts are restless till they find rest in Thee."[7]

Sehnsucht is that inscrutable ache to be at home, inside the fold of our Father's arms, safely returned to the garden and peacefully ensconced there in the fellowship of our brother Jesus. Not all will make it—many will drug the longing or deny it or deify it until their dying breath, launching out from this familiar unknown to pure terrors on the other side.

I once shared the saving message of Christ with a married couple, each on their deathbed at the same time. The wife was eager for home and sought refuge in the arms of Jesus. The husband had spent his life shaking his fist at God and was determined to go out the same way. He could not receive the good news. But his wife heard the good news as the answer to all her longing. Weak from cancer, a mere shell of her former self, as her body gave limply

---

[7] Augustine, *The Confessions of Saint Augustine*, trans. J. G. Pilkington (Edinburgh: T&T Clark, 1876), 1:1.

away, her spirit was flung powerfully into the arms of her Father. A daughter had come home for the first time.

And so we learn in the Scriptures that "the sum of the gospel embassy is to reconcile us to God."[8]

THE GOSPEL OF ADOPTION

There is a peculiar tension in the biblical narrative of redemption, a *depth* if you will, to our state apart from Christ before God. As already asserted, in one sense we are cast as lost children, foreknown by God before we are even born and loved by him from eternity past, and therefore predestined to be brought back into the fold. But in another sense, we are cast as total foreigners to God's fold—aliens and strangers, even rebels and enemies. The biblical characterization of our lostness is just as fully orbed as its characterization of Christ's goodness. In Ephesians 2:1–3, for instance, we learn that apart from Christ we are both dead and following the world, the Devil, and our appetites (which is quite a lot of activity for someone who is dead).

Yet we learn that the resolution to this tension—simultaneously a lost child of God and a rebellious stranger to God—emanates from God himself, who both hates and loves. What are we yearning for, groaning for? Our adoption as sons, according to Romans 8:23. And what makes enemies into sons is God himself, who according to Romans 8:14–15 leads us with his Spirit, the Spirit of adoption who translates for us our inner groaning to the cry of "Abba! Father!"

Deep in the foreknowledge of God is the reconciling difference between a fist shaken at the Father and an open hand upheld for his clasping. Proceeding from the Father is the Spirit who gives us the ears to know the voice of our brother-shepherd Jesus (John 10:27). Only in the complex depths of the triune godhead are wrath-owed enemies also love-won children. Isn't adoption too wonderful?

---

[8] John Calvin, *Institutes of the Christian Religion*, ed. John T. McNeill, trans. Ford Lewis Battles, 2 vols. (Philadelphia: Westminster, 1960), 2:739.

I will sow her for myself in the land.
And I will have mercy on No Mercy,
  and I will say to Not My People, "You are my people";
  and he shall say, "You are my God." (Hos. 2:23)

God takes people who are not his and makes them his. He makes friends with strangers, with enemies (John 15:15)! John Murray writes, "Adoption, as the term clearly implies, is an act of transfer from an alien family into the family of God himself. This is surely the apex of grace and privilege."[9]

God turns rebels into family. He does this in deep love before time began (Eph. 1:5), through meticulous sovereignty throughout the old covenant (Rom. 9:4), by abundant grace in the new covenant offering of Christ (Gal. 4:4–5), and with affectionate power in the Spirit's ongoing mission (Gal. 4:6). He is still on the surface of the deep, calling out order from the formless void of our hearts. And in this wonder is another incomprehensible wonder, namely that the Spirit's conversion of us godward is characterized as both adoption *and* rebirth.

When God adopts us into his family, he is not simply declaring us his children—he is actually making us his children. The Spiritual work of regeneration begins the Spiritual work of progressive sanctification, in which we are not just imputed Christ's righteousness but imparted it, as well. Knowing this, then, when we read 1 John 3:1—"See what kind of love the Father has given to us, that we should be called children of God"—we hear it as it is, a call to stagger in worship. Lewis Smedes tracks the story of Paul's reconciliation and similarly exults:

> Paul ran from Christ; Christ pursued and overtook him. Paul resisted Christ; Christ disarmed him. Paul persecuted Christ; Christ converted him. Paul was an alien; Christ made him a member of the family. Paul was an enemy; Christ made him a friend. Paul was "in the flesh"; Christ set him "in the Spirit." Paul was under the law; Christ set him in grace. Paul was dead; Christ made him alive to God. How does one give reasons for this? He

---

[9]John Murray, *Redemption Accomplished and Applied* (Grand Rapids, MI: Eerdmans, 1955), 134.

does not give reasons; he sings, "Blessed be God who blessed us . . . even as he chose us in him."[10]

Reasons? We don't need no stinking reasons. God's goal is to glorify himself, to make his name great. There's your reason. Because he is love (1 John 4:8) and wants to love. The heart wants what it wants. And God's heart wants people who hate him. He wants them stirred, turned, cleansed, and filled.

My religion professor in college, the late, great M. B. Jackson, used to say, quoting somebody he never cited, "Why, oh why, did God choose the Jews?" He would then take us to Deuteronomy 7:6–9, where we read:

> For you are a people holy to the LORD your God. The LORD your God has chosen you to be a people for his treasured possession, out of all the peoples who are on the face of the earth. It was not because you were more in number than any other people that the LORD set his love on you and chose you, for you were the fewest of all peoples, but it is because the LORD loves you and is keeping the oath that he swore to your fathers, that the LORD has brought you out with a mighty hand and redeemed you from the house of slavery, from the hand of Pharaoh king of Egypt. Know therefore that the LORD your God is God, the faithful God who keeps covenant and steadfast love with those who love him and keep his commandments, to a thousand generations.

Here is salvation by grace alone in the thick of the Torah. God did not consecrate Israel because of their numbers, their strength, or even their goodness. He did it because he did it. He did it out of love and out of his sacred prerogative.

Likewise, God does not save us because of anything in us. Woe to us when we think this! He chose us because he loves us. And he loves us because he chooses to, because he has set his love on us. He has set his designs on us, for no reason originating in ourselves. Isn't adoption unbelievably wonderful!

We see this pattern of gracious condescension in adoption throughout the Old Testament narrative and well into the New. To

---

[10] Lewis B. Smedes, *Union with Christ* (Grand Rapids, MI: Eerdmans, 1983), 86–87.

accomplish his saving purposes and magnify his sovereign grace, God chooses the younger brothers, the shepherd boys, the schemers, the dreamers, the ghetto dwellers and cats from the other side of the tracks, the imprisoned, the impotent, the impatient, the foreigners, the fakers, the fighters, the short-tempered, the hypersensitive, the deep feelers, the dum-dums, the dullards, and the dry bones. So that in all things he might be glorified in saying to Not My People, "You are *so* my people. Yes, even you." Isn't adoption astounding?

Matt Chandler tells a powerful story about taking an unbelieving friend to an evangelistic event:

> The preacher took the stage, and disaster ensued. I don't know how else to describe the sermon. There was very little Bible in it. He gave us a lot of statistics about STDs. There was a lot of, "You don't want syphilis, do you?" and, "It's all fun and games until you've got herpes on your lip." And in the middle of all this moralistic fearmongering, his big illustration was to take out a single red rose. He smelled the rose dramatically on stage, caressed its petals, and talked about how beautiful this rose was and how it had been fresh cut that day. In fact, he said, it was such a beautiful rose that he wanted all of us to see and smell it. So he threw the rose out into the crowd, and he encouraged everyone to pass it around. We were sitting toward the back of the auditorium of a thousand, and it made its way to us, all while he kept preaching. As he neared the end of his message, he asked for the rose back. And, of course, when he got it back in his hands, it was broken and drooping, and the petals were falling off. He held up this now-ugly rose for all to see, and his big finish was this: "Now who in the world would want *this*? Who would want this rose now? Would you be proud of this rose? Is this rose lovely?" His words and his tone were merciless.
>
> About a week or two later, Kim didn't show up for class. She didn't show up for class for a week. I called and left several messages but couldn't get hold of her. After about three weeks, I began to get nervous. I wondered if she had dropped out of school. She had a dark past, and I wondered if she had fallen back into some of her old habits. Then I got a phone call from a woman who claimed to be Kim's mom. Kim had been in an accident and

had been in the hospital right across the street from the university. So I hung up the phone with her mom, and I walked over to her hospital room. She was all bandaged up, and her face was still swollen. She had fallen out of a car that was going 70 miles an hour and had struck her head on the concrete and fractured her skull. The swelling wasn't so extensive as to cause long-term damage, but it did cause enough damage to keep her hospitalized for several weeks.

In the middle of our conversation, seemingly out of nowhere, she asked me, "Do you think I'm a dirty rose?" My heart sank inside of me, and I began to explain to her that the whole weight of the gospel of Jesus Christ is that Jesus wants the rose! It's Jesus's desire to save, redeem, and restore the dirty rose.[11]

The Father looks through the annals of history future, and we hold up our best and brightest. These are the heroes! These are the wunderkinds! These are worthy, we say. But God bypasses the lifestyles of the rich and famous, the halls of majesty and masters, in order to pick out the slaves, the scrubs, the sullied. "God chose what is foolish in the world to shame the wise; God chose what is weak in the world to shame the strong" (1 Cor. 1:27). He takes poor beggars and poor beggars only, the ratty and tired, the angry and the dirty, and he makes joyful sons and daughters out of them. Christian, he has looked through time to see you at your worst, and he says, because of Christ, "I'll take that one. This is my beloved child, in whom I am well pleased."

He puts the Spirit of adoption in us, by whose power we cry out to God as our Father, and as quickly as we realize our shame, he is covering it in the perfect righteousness of his only begotten Son. Because the Father has granted us new birth, adopting us as his own, we become joint-heirs with his Son:

> The Spirit himself bears witness with our spirit that we are children of God, and if children, then heirs—heirs of God and fellow heirs with Christ, provided we suffer with him in order that we may also be glorified with him. (Rom. 8:16–17)

---

[11] Matt Chandler, *The Explicit Gospel* (Wheaton, IL: Crossway, 2012), 207–8.

The riches of the Son belong to us now. The promise of exaltation purchased by his saving work is transferred to our account. All the Son has, he shares with us as his siblings. Consequently, if we are in Christ, we are as secure as Christ is. "For he who sanctifies and those who are sanctified all have one source. That is why he is not ashamed to call them brothers" (Heb. 2:11). In the love of adoption, the Son boasts to have us in the family and the Father calls us "the apple of his eye" (Zech. 2:8).

THE GOSPEL OF UNION WITH CHRIST

If adoption shows us the Father's heart for us, union with his Son shows us the shape of that heart. Many rightly consider the notion of the Christian's union with Christ as the sum of God's saving work. John Murray, for instance, writes that "union with Christ is really the central truth of the whole doctrine of salvation"[12] and that "it underlies every aspect of redemption both in its accomplishment and in its application."[13] Calvin affords union with Christ "the highest degree of importance."[14] Lewis Smedes holds that union with Christ is "at once the center and circumference of authentic human existence."[15] They go on and on, and so could we.[16]

The believer's union with Christ is everywhere in the New Testament Scriptures as the culmination of our union with Adam that is evident everywhere in the Old Testament. We see it implicitly in the phrase "in him" or "in Christ," which is not a simple phrase of spiritual sentimentality—such as one might use to sign off at the end of a correspondence—but rather a constant rhetorical leitmotif putting before our eyes ever-presently the sum and purpose of God's saving work in Christ: to bind us together with him.

The major analogy Jesus gives to explain his union with us is found in John 15:4–5:

---

[12] Murray, *Redemption Accomplished*, 161.
[13] Ibid., 165.
[14] Calvin, *Institutes*, 1:737.
[15] Smedes, *Union with Christ*, xii.
[16] See a rundown of more quotes on the importance of union with Christ at Justin Taylor, "Union with Christ: A Crash Course," *Between Two Worlds* (blog), February 9, 2011, http://thegospelcoalition.org/blogs/justintaylor/2011/02/09/union-with-christ-a-crash-course/.

> Abide in me, and I in you. As the branch cannot bear fruit by
> itself, unless it abides in the vine, neither can you, unless you
> abide in me. I am the vine; you are the branches. Whoever abides
> in me and I in him, he it is that bears much fruit, for apart from
> me you can do nothing.

The vine/branch relationship correlates to a saving relationship
with Jesus. He is in us, and we are in him. We are united with him
as branches are to the vine. To be cut from the vine is to be a dead
branch. To be united with the vine is to have life (and to bear fruit).

We see the union concept laid out theologically in Romans
6:3–11:

> Do you not know that all of us who have been baptized into
> Christ Jesus were baptized into his death? We were buried there-
> fore with him by baptism into death, in order that, just as Christ
> was raised from the dead by the glory of the Father, we too might
> walk in newness of life.
>
> For if we have been united with him in a death like his, we
> shall certainly be united with him in a resurrection like his. We
> know that our old self was crucified with him in order that the
> body of sin might be brought to nothing, so that we would no
> longer be enslaved to sin. For one who has died has been set free
> from sin. Now if we have died with Christ, we believe that we
> will also live with him. We know that Christ, being raised from
> the dead, will never die again; death no longer has dominion over
> him. For the death he died he died to sin, once for all, but the
> life he lives he lives to God. So you also must consider yourselves
> dead to sin and alive to God in Christ Jesus.

The gist of Paul's exposition of union with Christ in this passage can be found in 2 Corinthians 5:21—"For our sake he made
him to be sin who knew no sin, so that in him we might become
the righteousness of God"—or 1 Corinthians 15:22—"For as in
Adam all die, so also in Christ shall all be made alive." The gist is
this: apart from Christ we are in Adam and therefore under eternal condemnation from God, but through Christ we are in Christ
and therefore under God's blessing of eternal life. In Adam is only

death; in Christ is only life. (The word *only* is very important in that last sentence.)

Let's return to Romans 6:3–11, however, and see how Paul proclaims the believer's union with Christ and connects it to assorted consequences. Arranging it as follows is very revealing and thoroughly thrilling:

- We are united with Christ; therefore his sacrificial death is our sacrificial death.
- We are united with Christ; therefore his burial is our burial.
- We are united with Christ; therefore his resurrection is our new life.
- We are united with Christ; therefore we will be reunited with him in our future resurrection.
- We are united with Christ; therefore his crucifixion is our death.
- We are united with Christ; therefore his life is our life.
- We are united with Christ; therefore death has no dominion over us just as it has no dominion over him.
- We are united with Christ; therefore we are alive to God.

The implications of union with Christ are mind-blowing. Christ's perfect obedience becomes our perfect obedience. Christ's sinlessness becomes our sinlesseness. His death, our death. His resurrection, our resurrection. His exaltation, our exaltation. His riches, our riches.

> See how rich believers are, they are matched into the crown of heaven;. and by virtue of the conjugal union all Christ's riches go to believers, communion is founded in union. Christ communicates his graces. . . . As long as Christ hath it, believers shall not want; and he communicates his privileges, justification, glorification: he settles a kingdom upon his spouse for her jointure. . . . This is a key to the apostle's riddle, 2 Cor. 6:10, "As having nothing, yet possessing all." By virtue of the marriage-union, the saints are interested in all Christ's riches.[17]

It is no wonder that the language of union is at all points connected to the various gospel benefits. The gospel creates the church,

---

[17] Thomas Watson, *Discourses on Important and Interesting Subjects* (Glasgow, Scotland: Blackie, Fullarton, and Co., 1829), 1:614.

which is called Christ's body. The gospel application of marriage, in which man and wife are reckoned one flesh, corresponds to Christ and his bride. The gospel is declared in the Lord's Supper, which is called his flesh and blood. The gospel proclaims our justification in Christ. It proclaims our sanctification in Christ. It proclaims our glorification in Christ. In Christ we live and move and have our being. Arthur Pink elaborates:

> Union with Christ is the foundation of all spiritual blessings, so that if there had been no connection with Him, there could be no regeneration, no justification, no sanctification, no glorification. It is so in the natural world—adumbrating the spiritual: sever one of the members from my physical body, and it is dead; only by its union with my person does it partake of life.[18]

Union with Christ is a beautiful, inseparable tangle. By God's grace, through the gift of faith, we are bound up with him and he with us for all eternity. He has hemmed us in; he has us covered:

- *Christ is in us.* (John 14:20; 17:23; Rom. 8:10–11; 2 Cor. 13:5; Col. 1:27)
- *Christ is over us.* (Rom. 9:5; 1 Cor. 11:3; Col. 1:18, 3:1; Heb. 3:6)
- *Christ is through us.* (Rom. 15:18; 2 Cor. 2:14; 5:20)
- *Christ is with us.* (Matt. 18:20; 28:20; Eph. 2:5–6; 2 Tim. 4:17)
- *Christ is under us.* (Luke 6:47–48; 20:17; Acts 4:11; 1 Cor. 3:11)
- *Christ is around us* (that is to say, we are in and through him). (John 14:6; 1 Cor. 8:6; 2 Cor. 3:4, 14; 5:17; Gal. 3:27; Heb. 7:25)

Christ is also before us and for us. He intercedes for us and advocates for us (Heb. 7:25; 1 John 2:1). The gospel so engulfs us in Christ, we are mystically indistinguishable from him, at least in terms of our spiritual state. In Colossians 3:3, Paul describes union as being "hidden with Christ in God." Because of our union with Christ, we are secured *to* God and secured *from* sin, death, and Satan, and all this for as long as Christ lives, which is forever.

The Devil comes to make his attack. "I will come in over the walls," he thinks, like Milton's Satan, but Jesus is there, our fortress and refuge. "I will sneak in through the back door," the accuser

---

[18] Arthur Pink, *Spiritual Union and Communion* (Lafayette, IN: Sovereign Grace, 2002), 9.

says. But Jesus is there, too, waiting for him. He tries the side, the front, burrowing from underneath. At every point Jesus is there. "Where did all these Jesuses come from?" the snake hisses, but there is only one Jesus, and he is mighty to save and he has us covered and nothing can snatch us from his powerful hand.

So considered, Thomas Boston writes, "To be united with Christ is the foundation of all happiness, and the richest privileges."[19] And even this is an understatement.

CHRIST, THE WAY BACK

Even the bigness of union with Christ is a reflection of the bigness of God's saving design. At every angle of the gospel's narrative stands God the Author. We are saved by his grace, not our works. We are saved not merely from disability but from his wrath. We are saved not through our goodness but through his Son's. We are saved not to wander but into reconciliation to him and the fold of heaven. We are saved not primarily for our glory but for his. In short? We are saved by God from God through God to God for God. The idea for our salvation is the Father's; the work of our salvation is the Son's; the dispensing of our salvation is the Spirit's. So that in all things God will get the glory.

God has forged the blazing diamond of union with Jesus Christ in order that he might be seen as preeminent but also as necessary and desirable. He is the way, the truth, and the life (John 14:6). *He* is stardust; *he* is golden.

After Adam and Eve's banishment, God put an angel at the gate of the garden to guard it with a fiery sword. Why? I think it's because there is no getting back to the garden the same way we went out. We disobeyed our way into fallenness, but we cannot obey our way into redemption. Yes, we've got to get inside again, but the way we came out is not the way for us back in. None of us will be justified by our works. But not because obedience isn't the way in, but because the way is blocked. Only Jesus can go in that way. Only Jesus, "having become as much superior to angels

---

[19] Thomas Boston, *An Illustration of the Doctrines of the Christian Religion* (Berwick, UK: W. Gracie and J. Rennison, 1804), 2:134.

as the name he has inherited is more excellent than theirs" (Heb. 1:4), bests the guard.

That way is not the way for us. But *the* Way is, because he can go that way. And if we are united to him, he carries us with him. Through him we have access to the holy place (Eph. 2:18; Heb. 4:16). In him and with him and through him and by him, we will make our way into the restored garden, the place both strange and familiar, the home we long for.

> Then the angel showed me the river of the water of life, as clear as crystal, flowing from the throne of God and of the Lamb down the middle of the great street of the city. On each side of the river stood the tree of life, bearing twelve crops of fruit, yielding its fruit every month. And the leaves of the tree are for the healing of the nations. No longer will there be any curse. The throne of God and of the Lamb will be in the city, and his servants will serve him. (Rev. 22:1–3 NIV)

We turn now to the gospel's bright shadow play of this world to come . . .

Chapter Nine

COSMIC REDEMPTION

"Thou *sword* of truth, *fly* swift and sure,
that evil die and good endure!"
—Disney's *Sleeping Beauty*

Just a hop, skip, and jump from my office is Mineral Springs Park, a tiny cutout in the tiny town of Middletown Springs, Vermont, where an old resort once stood. In the olden days, local entrepreneurs boasted of the mineral springs' healing propertics, and people would come from all over the world to stay at the hotel and bathe in the water. Some enterprising souls started bottling the stuff for distribution. The spring is still there, of course, still bubbling up through a couple of marble slabs beneath a wooden gazebo and feeding into the winding Poultney River that flows through the park. And the stone foundation of the hotel bridge is still there, but the hotel is gone, replaced by ever-encroaching Vermont woodlands and a few historical markers.

When the weather's not prohibitive, I will sometimes walk from the church to the park, sit on the bench above the springs, and listen to the wind through the trees and the rush of the water. Nobody told me the grass was different in Vermont before I moved here. I've lived around woods (in northwest Houston, Texas, and in Nashville, Tennessee), and I've been to plenty of forests in various travels, but there's something special about New England forests. The trees are different. They're wetter, more vibrant. They have character and long memories, like Tolkien's Ents. I've never seen a greener green than in these *Verts Monts*. And when fall comes, setting the mountains ablaze with autumnal fire, the spectrum from gold to red declares the refining glory of God. The air is spicy with crushed apples and fireplace smoke and hunter's cooked quarry. Then the long New England winter arrives, burying everything in white, and the place gets stiller, quieter, on the edge of its frosty seat throughout the long hush to hear the first snap of spring thaw. That's when the sap starts running.

This place is ancient but ripe with the new. In Mineral Springs Park, any time of the year, I sit expectant. As if a talking beaver may lumber out at any minute, bringing news of Aslan's movements in the land. I can feel the deep magic there.

Many others do as well, and in many other places, and I've often wondered if there's a correlation between environmental largesse and the sort of hippy-dippy New Age cultures that seem to predominate around them. Pagan, pantheistic, and spiritualist religions proliferate in my neck of the woods, as they do in the Pacific Northwest and in the American Southwest. Why do you think that is?

I think it's precisely because the natural world is so undeniably and overwhelmingly beautiful in these places.

This thought was triggered in my mind one Sunday when one of our teenagers was presenting his testimony of a solo trek in the mountains of upstate New York over the summer. While flipping through projected photographs of his many hikes, he said to the congregation, "When you're in the mountains you realize, 'Yeah, I'm insignificant.'" That reminded me of something Matt Chandler once said: "Nobody ever stood at the base of the Rocky Mountains, looking up, and said, 'Remember that time in high school when I could bench three hundred pounds?'"

For many people—not all, of course—living in naturally beautiful places heightens the spiritual senses. So I wonder if the reason we see so many New Agers and what-not in these specific areas has something to do with the way the grandeur of God's creation has triggered in them a sense of the numinous—"Yes," they reason, struck small by the majesty of the mountains or the roaring of the oceans or the mystery of the desert, "there is something larger, more meaningful, more spiritual than me in the world"—while the rebellion of their heart has triggered in them a spiritual knee-jerk response of self-assertion in occultism. Perhaps New Agey-ness is a way of offsetting the pain of undeniable smallness.

But in the woods of Vermont I don't feel small so much as part of a bigger whole. Reality seems heightened there, stripped of man's artifice and brimming with God's artistry. For all the blessings of common grace we receive from the ongoing and rapid advances in technology, one thing we have struggled to receive from ever-morphing gadgets and gizmos is a sense of awe over God and a sense of expectation about what he may do next.

"Behold, I am making all things new," declares Jesus Christ (Rev. 21:5). The same promise is made by the inventors of electronic doodads. But only Jesus is telling the truth.

His renewing work killed him. But that is the way it's supposed to work. Disobedience unto death is undone by obedience unto death, and only Jesus was Man enough to do that. Crushed by the weight of the cross, pinned there by envy and nails, stricken and open, he achieved victory most epic. The veil between heaven and earth tore, the grave gave up its dead, the universe, tightly wound in its own burial shroud, rapidly unravels. Can you feel it shaking? "Truly this man was the Son of God!" (Mark 15:39).

And so the Scriptures tell us that Jesus Christ is the radiance of God's glory (Heb. 1:3) and that the heavens declare the glory of God (Ps. 19:1), that the glory of God is evident in creation (Rom. 1:20). For this reason, John Calvin spoke of creation as "the theater of God's glory," a worldwide proscenium under which the wonder of Christ was to be beheld, projected, and enjoyed. Every jot and tittle of general revelation is meant as an arrow to the special revelation of the living and sovereign Word of God. Mark Talbot writes:

> In the *Institutes*, "this most glorious theater" means our universe, and the works referred to are God's work in creation and providence. Like an architect who manifests his greatness in every feature of an opera house from the grand sweep of its tiered balconies to his little touches with its light switches, so God reveals and "daily discloses [his glory] in the whole workmanship of the universe" from the splendor of the heavens to the shape and structure of the toenails on an infant's feet.[1]

---

[1] Mark Talbot, "Sin and Suffering in Calvin's World and Ours" in *With Calvin in the Theater of God*, ed. John Piper and David Mathis (Wheaton, IL: Crossway, 2010), 53.

The story told in the theater is set in the theater itself—which is to say, God says something through creation about the gospel that says something about creation—and Jesus is the central player in the whole shebang. The entire Bible unfolds this intricate story for us, first in shadows, finally in blazing light.

THE PENTATEUCH AS WITNESS TO COSMIC REDEMPTION

In the beginning, the universe did not need redemption. But it is an inscrutable wonder to think of God's mind as he hung stars, separated land from sea, drew forth vegetation, and finally created man and woman, holding inside of it the future fall and ensuing necessity of salvation for it all. In any event, he made it all and declared it all good. Genesis is where God makes everything blessed, and it's also where we bring the curse. But as early as Genesis 3:15 we see the foreshadow of the reversal to come. God curses the serpent:

> I will put enmity between you and the woman,
>   and between your offspring and her offspring;
> he shall bruise your head,
>   and you shall bruise his heel.

Biblical scholars call this the *protoevangelion*, which means "first gospel." Barely into the story, we've messed everything up, but very quickly God gives us a glimpse of Golgotha, where evil bruises the heel of Christ, which is simultaneously bruising evil's head. Genesis 3:15 is a matryoshka doll of gospel vision, because encased in this first gospel is the crucifixion, and in the crucifixion is encased the last gospel of the finality of Satan's defeat. But more on that later.

After the curse, things spiral out of control quickly. From Cain's murder of Abel in Genesis 4 to Moses's denial in death of seeing the Promised Land in Deuteronomy 34, the story of God's covenant people in the earliest of days is full of blatant evil and unfulfilled longing. Woven into this narrative fabric are multiple threads of God's gospel vision for creation. In the fall, creation is cursed. But in the various gospel provisions, there is promise of restoration.

There is Noah's rainbow, of course (Gen. 9:12–17). The destruction of the world by flood is a foreshadow of God's wrath in judgment in the day to come, but God's covenant people are safe and secure, emerging from the torrent to a cleansed creation. "After the flood, all the colors came out," Bono sings, and I assume he is bringing to mind the text as much symbolically as he is literally.[2] In Noah's story, God gives us a peek at his future plan to restore creation in, through, and after the day of judgment. And he is showing us the relationship between mankind and creation, our interdependence with each other and our mutual dependence on the beneficence of the Creator. Lesslie Newbigin elaborates:

> In raising his beloved Son from the dead, God has given the pledge and the foretaste of his unconquerable grace in kindness and patience toward the world which rejects him. In the resurrection of Jesus, the original covenant with creation and with all human life, the covenant with Noah and his descendants, is reaffirmed. The world of human culture rejects God and is under God's judgments. But God in his patient and long-suffering love sustains the created world, and the world of human culture, in order that there may still be time and space for repentance and for the coming into being of the new creation within the womb of the old. God still cherishes and sustains the world of creation and culture, in spite of its subjection to illusion and vanity. The covenant with Noah and its rainbow sign refer explicitly to one of the most basic elements in human culture, namely the work of the farmer who cultivates the wilderness in order that it may bring forth food for human beings (Gen. 8:22). Here the interdependence of human beings and nature, and the dependence of both on the grace of God, are at their most manifest.[3]

When God establishes his covenant with Abraham, we see two important details: the covenant is everlasting and it involves the land of Canaan (Gen. 17:1–14). This is another narrative example of

---

[2] U2, "Beautiful Day," 2000.
[3] Lesslie Newbigin, *The Gospel in a Pluralist Society* (Grand Rapids, MI: Eerdmans, 1989), 194.

God's plan in the gospel for creation. We see still more each time God renames his people (Abram to Abraham, Sarai to Sarah, Jacob to Israel, etc.) and each time God's people name and rename their geographic locations. They are taking dominion, sure, but they are also commemorating God's saving activity point by point, staking gospel claim on the land. Jacob, post-tussle with the Lord, dubbing the scene "Peniel" is but one example (Gen. 32:30).

Later, Egypt is in famine and God's man Joseph rises to prominence through persecution. Despite his ability to deny brothers and aliens alike, he opens the storehouse of grain to provide for all (Genesis 41–45). Sound familiar? He is the shadow and lesser Jesus who forgives those who hate him and opens the storehouse of his goodness for all who seek him. As it will be in the final day, God's healing of the land through the gracious benevolence of his appointee declares his concern for its restoration.

Genesis gives way to Exodus, where God demonstrates his use of creation in burning bushes, bloody rivers, falling frogs, pillars of cloud and fire, parting seas, and raining manna. God is sovereign over nature's order and chaos; he orchestrates it! And all so that the Israelites may be moved from a foreign land to the promised one. And thus Exodus is a historical narrative that is nonetheless metaphorical of the metanarrative of the gospel. God's judgment is coming to fallen creation, but his plan is not to evacuate his people, but transfer them, through the administration of the true and better Moses, into the Land of Promise, the true and better land. The Israelites sing a worship song with these lyrics:

> Now are the chiefs of Edom dismayed;
>> trembling seizes the leaders of Moab;
>> all the inhabitants of Canaan have melted away.
> Terror and dread fall upon them;
>> because of the greatness of your arm, they are still as a stone,
> till your people, O Lord, pass by,
>> till the people pass by whom you have purchased.
> You will bring them in and plant them on your own mountain,
>> the place, O Lord, which you have made for your abode,

the sanctuary, O Lord, which your hands have established.
The LORD will reign forever and ever. (Ex. 15:15–18)

We must keep in mind that the Israelites did not chiefly think
"heaven" when singing of God's reigning forever and ever on and
over his own mountain—at least, not the sort of heaven we typically think of. They are singing of his *manifest reign* over all creation, of his establishing his reign over and in the midst of his
people. Moses, after all, was not assumed to the spirit world to
meet with God, but "merely" ascended Mount Sinai. God met him
there, and we may say in some real sense that Moses was going
to heaven in these encounters, or rather that heaven was coming
to him, but not in the sense that Enoch or Elijah or Jesus went to
heaven (Gen. 5:24; 2 Kings 2:11). What the Exodus people are longing for is what all God's people longed for throughout the biblical
storyline: God's coming to earth in presence and power, in fellowship with his people as in the days of Eden. The place where God
is, *that* is heaven. "Let this place be that place," they are saying.

God sends bread out of heaven and water out of rocks (Exodus
16–17). Only the shortsighted would not see glimpses of the restoration of creation in these miracles. Moses begins making his
mountainous treks, and he descends with the Law. And just as
the gospel visions for individuals' reconciliation to God, individuals' reconciliation to each other, and individuals' reconciliation
together corporately to God are tucked into the features of the
Law, so is God's gospel vision for the restoration of creation. We
see it in the promise of Canaan (Ex. 23:20–33), the Levitical regulations concerning bodily discharges and sickness and diseases,
and especially in the way God commands humane treatment of
animals (Deut. 22:1–4, 6–7, 10; 25:4) and Sabbath rest for the land
(Lev. 25:4–5; 26:34).

God is giving through the Law a vision for creation as it should
be and will be. "Whoever is righteous has regard for the life of his
beast, but the mercy of the wicked is cruel," Proverbs 12:10 tells
us. None of this means we aren't meant to use creation, but there
is a difference between use and abuse, dominion and exploitation,

stewardship and spending. Practice of the first set flows from an understanding of what God means to do with animals and land—not destroy but renew.

The establishment of the tabernacle is perhaps the strongest sign in the books of Moses that God's plan for creation is his inhabitancy of it as sovereign. God tabernacles with his people then; he tabernacles with us now in his Spirit; and he will tabernacle with his people again upon Christ's appearing.

THE HISTORICAL BOOKS AS WITNESS TO COSMIC REDEMPTION

Joshua's book begins with YHWH commissioning Joshua (Jesus's namesake) to assume the Land of Promise. He pronounces gospel: "The LORD your God is with you wherever you go" (Josh. 1:9). And because the gospel of God's covenant promises are true, these commands can be obeyed:

> Now therefore arise, go over this Jordan, you and all this people, into the land that I am giving to them, to the people of Israel. Every place that the sole of your foot will tread upon I have given to you, just as I promised to Moses. From the wilderness and this Lebanon as far as the great river, the river Euphrates, all the land of the Hittites to the Great Sea toward the going down of the sun shall be your territory. No man shall be able to stand before you all the days of your life. Just as I was with Moses, so I will be with you. I will not leave you or forsake you. Be strong and courageous, for you shall cause this people to inherit the land that I swore to their fathers to give them. (Josh. 1:2–6)

The Land of Promise is not incidental to God's saving purposes. It is part and parcel of them. God has chosen and set apart a people by his grace, and this people is to receive him by and follow him in faith. The repeated blessing of this covenant relationship is inheritance of the creation. Joshua's book is a chronicle of conquest.

It does not last for long, however, for even as the Israelites take dominion over the land, they must do so under the curse of Adam. Creation is groaning and they along with it. As the idolatrous Canaanites flourish, the Israelites do not vanquish them but attempt to cohabitate. But we can never make peace with idols. "What partnership has righteousness with lawlessness?" Paul asks. "Or what fellowship has light with darkness?" (2 Cor. 6:14). In submitting to an unequal yoking, the children of God fail to complete the conquest. Departure from worship of God alone is not far off. Even as God raises up judges to govern in the absence of Joshua's courageous leadership, the Israelites go whoring after other gods.

The curse proliferates. "In those days there was no king in Israel. Everyone did what was right in his own eyes" (Judg. 17:6). But the hope of gospel renewal remains. It is there bright and cosmic in this dark book, in Deborah and Barak's song in Judges 5, in Gideon's defeat of Midian (the result of which, we are told, is that "the land had rest forty years," Judg. 8:28), and in Jephthah's deliverance of the covenant lands (Judg. 11:1–22). In the midst of the vilest of sins, the most pervasive idolatry, and rampant disregard for human life comes the promise: "And all that the LORD our God has dispossessed before us, we will possess" (Judg. 11:24).

The vision of creation's renewal continues through the historical saga. For Boaz to redeem Ruth is also to redeem the "parcel of land" (Ruth 4:3). They are a package deal. When David, another shadow and lesser Jesus, defeats Goliath and thus the Philistines, God's people plunder the enemy camp and possess it (1 Samuel 17). When the ark of the covenant is placed in a habitation, David sings of *creation's* response:

> Sing to the LORD, all the earth!
>> Tell of his salvation from day to day. . . .
>> Tremble before him, all the earth;
>> yes, the world is established; it shall never be moved.
> Let the heavens be glad, and let the earth rejoice,
>> and let them say among the nations, "The LORD reigns!"
> Let the sea roar, and all that fills it;
>> let the field exult, and everything in it!
> Then shall the trees of the forest sing for joy
>> before the LORD, for he comes to judge the earth.
> Oh give thanks to the LORD, for he is good;
>> for his steadfast love endures forever! (1 Chron. 16:23, 30–34)

If creation groans for its redemption, surely it will sing when it comes.

When David dies, his son, Solomon, makes good on his father's dream to build YHWH a temple, that he might inhabit the Land of Promise among his people forever (1 Kings 8:13). King Josiah leads a reformation, and the land is blessed. Ezra and Nehemiah see the rebuilding of the temple and the city walls after the destruction at the hands of the Chaldeans, and God's people reconstitute under numerous social reforms. The book of Esther shows us God's concern for the political and the civic, for justice in the community of earth, and for the preservation of righteousness therein.

The resounding theme of the Bible's historical books is that God's covenant promises are everlasting and that he intends for his people to hallow his name among his creation; that he has these intentions in the face of and in spite of our constant sin is a testament to his grace in the gospel of Jesus. This becomes clearer the further we go into the biblical story.

THE WISDOM BOOKS AS WITNESS TO COSMIC REDEMPTION

The suffering Job is emphatic:

> For I know that my Redeemer lives,
>   and at the last he will stand upon the earth.
> And after my skin has been thus destroyed,
>   yet in my flesh I shall see God,
> whom I shall see for myself,
>   and my eyes shall behold, and not another.
> My heart faints within me! (Job 19:25–27)

What is his vision? A restored body on a restored earth beholding the Son of God standing upon that earth. Even here in the Old Testament we do not foresee that "dying and going to heaven" is the end of the story but just the beginning of the end of the story. The true climax is a story of its own, a happily ever after without conflict or end, in which Jesus Christ "stands upon the earth" and we behold his glory with renewed eyes and praise him with renewed flesh.

This vision is glimpsed all over the Psalms. Psalm 104:30 says God will "renew the face of the ground." Psalm 102:26 says he will change the heavens and the earth "like a robe." Psalm 37 includes a few choice phrases: "those who wait for the LORD shall inherit the land" (v. 9); "the meek shall inherit the land and delight them-selves in abundant peace" (v. 11); and "The righteous shall inherit the land and dwell upon it forever" (v. 29), among others. Psalm 96:10–13 is a particularly stirring forecast:

> Say among the nations, "The LORD reigns!
>   Yes, the world is established; it shall never be moved;
>   he will judge the peoples with equity."
> Let the heavens be glad, and let the earth rejoice;
>   let the sea roar, and all that fills it;
>   let the field exult, and everything in it!
> Then shall all the trees of the forest sing for joy
>   before the LORD, for he comes,
>   for he comes to judge the earth.
> He will judge the world in righteousness,
>   and the peoples in his faithfulness.

"For he comes to judge the earth" should not be seen strictly in terms of "judging in wrath" but more generally as "judging as ruling sovereign." The groaning earth is exulting in this vision, glad and joyful that the Lord is coming to finally and eternally establish his harmonizing sovereignty.

The notion of cosmic redemption and our glorified presence in it appears early on even in the book of Proverbs. "For the upright will inhabit the land, and those with integrity will remain in it" (Prov. 2:21). And later: "The righteous will never be removed, but the wicked will not dwell in the land" (Prov. 10:30).

The Teacher of Ecclesiastes tells us "A generation goes, and a generation comes, but the earth remains forever" (Eccles. 1:4). Of course, the vision of impending refinement in 2 Peter 3:7 lets us know that the earth will not continue unchanged. But that this earth will somehow endure is nevertheless the poetic vision the wisdom books offer us. But the prophets, even in their apocalyptic grandeur, spell it out for us most clearly.

THE PROPHETS AS WITNESS TO COSMIC REDEMPTION

The Exodus people's longing for God's presence among his people becomes more detailed and vivid in the vision of the prophets as they wait for the Messiah. And what the Messiah will do is simply staggering. A sampling from Isaiah:

> For behold, I create new heavens
>   and a new earth,
> and the former things shall not be remembered
>   or come into mind. (Isa. 65:17)

> For behold, the LORD will come in fire,
>   and his chariots like the whirlwind,
> to render his anger in fury,
>   and his rebuke with flames of fire.
> For by fire will the LORD enter into judgment,
>   and by his sword, with all flesh;
>   and those slain by the LORD shall be many. . . .
> For as the new heavens and the new earth
>   that I make
> shall remain before me, says the LORD,
>   so shall your offspring and your name remain.
> From new moon to new moon,
>   and from Sabbath to Sabbath,
> all flesh shall come to worship before me,
> declares the LORD. (Isa. 66:15–16, 22–23)

Isaiah 40 is very powerful, as well.

Jeremiah 31 offers a parallel vision, the day when God reconstitutes his covenant people, wiping away all fear and pain and grief, and establishes them in the land of their ancestors with himself appearing among them. Jeremiah 23 provides a similar picture.

Ezekiel 39:28–29 says this about the restoration to come:

Then they shall know that I am the LORD their God, because I sent them into exile among the nations and then assembled them into their own land. I will leave none of them remaining among the nations anymore. And I will not hide my face anymore from them, when I pour out my Spirit upon the house of Israel, declares the Lord GOD.

Ezekiel's prophecy ends with the vision of a holy city on the earth, and its name will be The Lord Is There (Ezek. 48:35).

Daniel is full of end-times visions. Here is a prophecy of Jesus's return to establish his reign upon the renewed earth:

I saw in the night visions,

> and behold, with the clouds of heaven
>   there came one like a son of man,
> and he came to the Ancient of Days
>   and was presented before him.
> And to him was given dominion
>   and glory and a kingdom,
> that all peoples, nations, and languages
>   should serve him;
> his dominion is an everlasting dominion,
>   which shall not pass away,
> and his kingdom one
>   that shall not be destroyed. (Dan. 7:13–14)

The visions continue into the minor prophets. Two of my favorite passages include Habakkuk 2:14 and Malachi 4. In the latter, the "sun of righteousness" is said to rise with healing in its wings (Mal. 4:2).

In the new covenant Gospels we come up close and personal with this healing sun.

THE MIRACLES AS WITNESS TO COSMIC REDEMPTION

As Jesus goes about declaring the coming of the kingdom of God in and through himself, he self-authenticates through signs and wonders. The cumulative testimony of the miracles is that Jesus is the end-all, be-all. And these works give us glimpses into the restoration of creation that is coming. They are signposts into that other world.

Jesus heals the sick, blind, and lame not just to demonstrate his power, but to signal the day when there will be no more of such things. When he restores the flesh of the lepers and even raises the dead, he is showing God's plan revealed in Isaiah 40:5:

> And the glory of the LORD shall be revealed,
>   and all flesh shall see it together,
>   for the mouth of the LORD has spoken.

When Jesus exorcises demons, multiplies fish and loaves, walks on water, and so on and so forth, he is showing how God's kingdom is coming to earth, how God's will will be done on earth as it is in heaven. He is giving people a foretaste of the day when all that exists on earth is God's kingdom, because heaven and earth will have been unified in a way that leaves no room for evil, pain, or lack.

These miracle signs culminate in Jesus's own resurrection, the catalyst for our future resurrection, habitation of the new earth, and the reversal of creation's curse. One of my favorite reflections on the bigness of this truth is found in Sally Lloyd-Jones's *Jesus Storybook Bible*:

> "Mary!"
>   Only one person said her name like that. She could hear her heart thumping. She turned around. She could just make out a figure. She shaded her eyes to see . . . and thought she was dreaming.
>   But she wasn't dreaming. She was seeing.
>   "Jesus!"
>   Mary fell to the ground. Sudden tears filled her eyes and great sobs shook her whole body, and all she wanted in that moment was to cling to Jesus and never let him go.
>   "You'll be able to hold on to me later, Mary," Jesus said gently, "and always be close to me. But now, go and tell the others that I'm alive!"

Mary ran and ran, all the way to the city. She had never run so fast or so far in all her life. She felt she could have run forever. She didn't even feel like her feet touched the ground. The sun seemed to be dancing and gleaming and bounding across the sky, racing with her and shining brighter than she could ever remember in the clear, fresh air.

And it seemed to her that morning, as she ran, almost as if the whole world had been made anew, almost as if the whole world was singing for joy—the trees, tiny sounds in the grass, the birds . . . her heart.

Was God really making everything sad come untrue? Was he making even death come untrue?[4]

The apostles then tease out for us the gospel of Jesus's kingdom. Peter writes, "But according to his promise we are waiting for new heavens and a new earth in which righteousness dwells" (2 Pet. 3:13). But we will look at Paul's revelations for the most direct instruction.

PAUL AS PROPHET OF COSMIC REDEMPTION

Creation is good (Gen. 1:4, 10, 12), but it is giving way now to its truer and better self. All because Jesus Christ died on the cross to forgive sinners and rose from the grave to purchase eternal life. What the gospel does is personal, yes, but also cosmic. The gospel of Jesus Christ is scaled to eternity. What the Bible shows us is that God saves sinners through the life, death, and resurrection of Jesus Christ, and this salvation is the primary and central piece of the whole redemptive puzzle, the big picture of which reveals that God is saving the world through the life, death, and resurrection of Jesus Christ. This is so that Jesus will be preeminent in our hearts, but also so that he will be seen as preeminent in the universe (Col. 1:18), so that our hearts will be at home in the universe. That feeling I get in Mineral Springs Park is a foretaste of this.

Paul makes this connection for us in Romans 8. In verses 1 and 2, he writes:

---

[4]Sally Lloyd-Jones, *The Jesus Storybook Bible* (Grand Rapids, MI: Zondervan, 2007), 314–17.

There is therefore now no condemnation for those who are in Christ Jesus. For the law of the Spirit of life has set you free in Christ Jesus from the law of sin and death.

What Christ did at the cross absorbs the wrath of God, serves as propitiation, and therefore removes condemnation from over our heads and really, truly, deeply sets us free. But it is for freedom that we are set free, so there is an accomplishment Christ's saving work leaves yet undone. Paul moves to this in verses 18–25:

For I consider that the sufferings of this present time are not worth comparing with the glory that is to be revealed to us. For the creation waits with eager longing for the revealing of the sons of God. For the creation was subjected to futility, not willingly, but because of him who subjected it, in hope that the creation itself will be set free from its bondage to corruption and obtain the freedom of the glory of the children of God. For we know that the whole creation has been groaning together in the pains of childbirth until now. And not only the creation, but we ourselves, who have the firstfruits of the Spirit, groan inwardly as we wait eagerly for adoption as sons, the redemption of our bodies. For in this hope we were saved. Now hope that is seen is not hope. For who hopes for what he sees? But if we hope for what we do not see, we wait for it with patience.

All of creation is groaning along with us—because of us—for its final freedom, its restoration to its former glory, the glory that is to be revealed. In verses 1–2, Paul says the gospel has set us free. In this passage he indicates that creation, and we with it, are still in some way hoping for freedom. This introduces the important idea of "inaugurated eschatology," which helps us see that as it pertains to Christ's finished work, we now live in a state of "already" and "not yet." Already we are free, but we are also not yet free. We are already adopted, but we are not yet adopted. We are already saved, but we are not yet saved.

Paul calls the already "the firstfruits of the Spirit." In the hope of eternal life, which we now have and later will also have, we were saved, are saved, and will be saved. Now we possess eternal life. Then we will enjoy it most fully forever.

Paul gets even more specific on this eschatological dynamic in 1 Corinthians 15. In verses 1–4, he writes:

> Now I would remind you, brothers, of the gospel I preached to you, which you received, in which you stand, and by which you are being saved, if you hold fast to the word I preached to you—unless you believed in vain. For I delivered to you as of first importance what I also received: that Christ died for our sins in accordance with the Scriptures, that he was buried, that he was raised on the third day in accordance with the Scriptures.

In verses 1–2 Paul shows how the gospel of verses 3–4 saved us (past), saves us (present), and is saving us (present-future). Then he takes the same turn he took in Romans 8, only this time with more details. In 1 Corinthians 15:20–28 he says that because of Christ's finished work in history, more specifically his resurrection, we receive the firstfruits of our future resurrection. Paul notes that what God is doing in this interim, in the "now," is putting more and more in subjection to Jesus, with the end result being "all things in subjection under him, that God may be all in all" (1 Cor. 15:28). Then, in verses 35–58, we discover something wonderful. What Christ accomplished on the cross and out of the tomb is becoming realized in history, the culmination of which will be the final vanquishing of sin and Satan, the complete conquer of death and corruption, the face-to-face reconciliation of God's children to their brother King Jesus. This blissful meeting will be glorified face to glorified face, as we receive in the end of "not yet" our resurrection bodies, immortal and incorruptible.

Where will we be? In heaven, yes. But we are not given new bodies—presumably like Jesus's, which was tangible and physical but Spiritual too, able to be touched and eat breakfast but also able to walk through locked doors and ascend to the place where God is—so that we can occupy an invisible place of disembodied bliss. We will be given new bodies to occupy the new creation.

The gospel creates all of this.

REVELATION AS WITNESS TO COSMIC REDEMPTION

Every student of theater, and a few of literature in general, know this very important rule of theatrical storytelling. If you introduce a gun in the first act (Gen. 3:15), it will be fired by the last (Rev. 20:1–10). God promised minutes after the fall that man would crush the head of the serpent, and minutes before the end, at just the right time, he will make good on this promise as the exalted Christ hurls Satan into the lake of fire forever after.

In Revelation 21, John recounts his vision of the new heaven and the new earth anticipated since the moment of the fall, promised in the days of the patriarchs, lamented over and groaned for in the covenant people's poetry, shadowed by the prophets, inaugurated by the incarnate Word, and instructed by the apostles. Heaven is coming to earth!

> Then I saw a new heaven and a new earth, for the first heaven and the first earth had passed away, and the sea was no more. And I saw the holy city, new Jerusalem, coming down out of heaven from God, prepared as a bride adorned for her husband. And I heard a loud voice from the throne saying, "Behold, the dwelling place of God is with man. He will dwell with them, and they will be his people, and God himself will be with them as their God. He will wipe away every tear from their eyes, and death shall be no more, neither shall there be mourning, nor crying, nor pain anymore, for the former things have passed away."
>
> And he who was seated on the throne said, "Behold, I am making all things new."
>
> Also he said, "Write this down, for these words are trustworthy and true." And he said to me, "It is done! I am the Alpha and the Omega, the beginning and the end. To the thirsty I will give from the spring of the water of life without payment. The one who conquers will have this heritage, and I will be his God and he will be my son."
>
> And I saw no temple in the city, for its temple is the Lord God the Almighty and the Lamb. And the city has no need of sun or moon to shine on it, for the glory of God gives it light, and its lamp is the Lamb. By its light will the nations walk, and the kings of the earth will bring their glory into it, and its gates will never

be shut by day—and there will be no night there. They will bring into it the glory and the honor of the nations. (Rev. 21:1–7, 22–26)

Hallelujah! What Christ has accomplished on the cross and out of the grave has purchased all creation back, redeeming us and it from sin and death. The sun of righteousness has risen with healing in its wings; it is *he*, the Light of the World, and he will be the sun of the new heavens and the new earth so that the entire earth will be filled with the knowledge of the glory of God as the waters cover the sea.

THE GOSPEL'S THICK HEAVEN

The last decade has seen the tremendous devastating power of the tsunami. First in Near East Asia, then in the Far East. Most recently we've seen the utter destruction in Japan. Creation groans for redemption, and we with it. We don't know exactly what natural phenomena or weather patterns will occupy the new heavens and the new earth, but our gospel gives us evidence that in the age to come, either the earth will be tsunami-proof or we will. Once heaven and earth are integrated, this place will gleam with the power of that place.

For now, we groan. For now, we expect. For now, we long. Because as the Bible shows us, every sliver of everything is ripe with its future self.

Several years ago Wim Wenders created a now-classic foreign film, *Wings of Desire*, in which an angel renounces his angel-ness to experience human romance with the woman he'd fallen in love with. (*Wings of Desire* was remade a few years later in the American film *City of Angels*, with Nicolas Cage and Meg Ryan.) One of the major conceits of *Wings of Desire* was that in his angelic form our lover saw the world—and we saw the film—in black and white and shades of gray. When he gave up his wings and became human, the film turns to color to reflect his now fully-realized vision.

This is backwards.

Only in the mind whose treasure is set on earth are the heavenlies seen as drab and the earth seen as glorious (by comparison). Our world *is* glorious, of course, because the skies declare the glory of God, the mountains and trees declare his majesty, and as Calvin reminds us, every blade of grass is meant to make us rejoice. But heaven is far, far better.

Our problem, then, is probably not that this fallen world is seen as too beautiful (I could argue it's not seen as beautiful enough, actually), but that we have a deficient view of heaven. It is more colorful than this world, not less. It is, as C. S. Lewis depicts it in *The Great Divorce*, thicker than our world.

Do you realize that Christ's glorified body is in the heavenly space? His is a body that is tangible, real, space-taking. It can eat food and be touched. But it can also pass through locked doors, *defy* matter and space. Elijah and Enoch are there, in their bodies in some real sense.

Heaven is not some thin place, some cosmic hyperbaric chamber for disembodied spirits only. It is realer, truer, grander. Lewis may have captured the best illustrative parallel of how heaven "works" with his Narnia stories. Narnia is a real place with its own time, space, matter, contents. Narnia is bigger than our world but nevertheless within our world, or at least accessible within our world. It is not outer space, it is inner space but outsized space. Bigger inside than it looks outside.

The staggering beauty of this realer reality is that heaven is not a holding pattern but an approaching land. Our own world is groaning for our and its redemption, and in the consummation of the kingdom at the swiftly coming return of our Lord, every nook and cranny of this world will be restored, covered with the glory of God. The new heavens and new earth will make this place more colorful, not less. Thicker, realer, truer, better. As I wrote in *Your Jesus Is Too Safe*, heaven's subsuming of fallen creation will be in "an eternal splash of glory the likes of which will make the aurora borealis look like a Lite Brite."[5]

Imagine there is a fuller range of more vibrant colors than our complete spectrum. Imagine a new creation. The Himalayas, the pink of dawn, Angel Falls, the emerald hills of Ireland, the

---

[5] Jared C. Wilson, *Your Jesus Is Too Safe: Outgrowing a Drive-Thru, Feel-Good Savior* (Grand Rapids, MI: Kregel, 2009), 35.

"deep magic" of England, the pearl of Sudan, the coral reefs of Australia, the secret wonders of the Chinese wilderness, the crystal beauty of the Arctic, Mineral Springs Park in Middletown Springs, Vermont—all pale signposts to the world that is coming.

We worship a God whose wonders we will marvel at for eternity, because eternity cannot exhaust his wonders. We've got a ten-dimensional Jesus in a heaven so heavy our thin space can't conceal it much longer; it must crash into this world. Maranatha!

Chapter Ten

THE CROSSWISE EXCELLENCIES OF CHRIST

"In Christ infinite greatness and infinite goodness meet together, and receive lustre and glory one from another. His greatness is rendered lovely by his goodness. The greater any one is without goodness, so much the greater evil; but when infinite goodness is joined with greatness, it renders it a glorious and adorable greatness."—Jonathan Edwards

In essence, the gospel of Jesus Christ is Jesus Christ himself. In substance, the gospel of Jesus Christ is a revelation of his infinite excellencies. The gospel would not be a gospel at all if it should deliver us from evil, make us good people, and bring us heaven—if it did all of this (and more)—apart from Jesus. The point of the deep gospel is the high exaltation of the Son of God:

> And he is before all things, and in him all things hold together. And he is the head of the body, the church. He is the beginning, the firstborn from the dead, that in everything he might be preeminent. (Col. 1:17–18)

It is from his fullness and none other that we receive grace upon grace (John 1:16). To study the gospel, then, in all its wonders and effects, is to better see "the glory of God in the face of Jesus Christ" (2 Cor. 4:6).

This is all that we might *love* him. That we might know his love and love him. What good will it be to see the lovely depths of the gospel but not see Jesus as lovely? The answer is, no good at all. The angels are fascinated by the gospel, but it is not for them. The demons know the gospel, but it is not for them. The gospel is for us, because Christ is for us, and until we love our Savior we do not have his gospel in our heart. "Everyone who believes that Jesus is the Christ has been born of God, and everyone who loves the Father loves whoever has been born of him" (1 John 5:1). For two chapters, John argues that saved people love others; he reasons so strongly that to say if we don't have love for each other, we don't know the love of God. How much more so ought knowing the love of God bring us to love of God's Son?

When I lived in Nashville, I participated in a pastors' "gospel group" with a few fellows, including my friend Ray Ortlund. One morning as we gathered in Ray's office, he proceeded to astound us simply by talking about his friend Jesus. I can't recapture the magic of Ray's words in those moments, can't do them justice. But as he spoke, the rest of us went slack-jawed. We felt small as Jesus got bigger and bigger and filled up the room. Ray told us how tall Jesus was (I think he said eight feet), what made him laugh, how easily he interacted with children, what his face looked like when angry. The insights continued for just a few minutes. Ray was "making things up," of course, but not really. He wasn't being silly or superstitious. He was telling us about his friend. I have heard and read others attempting to personalize Jesus this way with much different effects. But in Ray's words were both a holy reverence, an awed fear of Jesus, and an affectionate, intimate familiarity. When Ray speaks of Jesus, I think to myself, "I want to know Jesus like that. I want to love him like that." Because Ray magnifies Jesus and adorns him with praise.

In Colossians 1:25–27 Paul says that Christ in us is the riches of the glory of the mystery of God's Word obscured for generations. He is not just the mystery revealed, but he is the mystery revealed as glory. And he is not just glory; he is the *riches* of glory. Christ himself is the all-surpassing treasure, but "the tested genuineness" of our faith is "more precious than gold," as well, because it results in love for the Savior we have yet to see face to face (1 Pet. 1:6–9).

Yet loving Jesus more and more requires looking at him as he is revealed in the Scriptures more and more, beholding him Spiritually in a real sense of his transforming glory. The author of Hebrews presents the dazzling Christ this way:

He is the radiance of the glory of God and the exact imprint of his nature, and he upholds the universe by the word of his power. After making purification for sins, he sat down at the right hand of the Majesty on high, having become as much superior to angels as the name he has inherited is more excellent than theirs. (Heb. 1:3–4)

As we have seen, the glory of God is the weightiness of his being, the sum of his attributes and character. This passage tells us that Jesus is the radiance of that weight and sum, which means that Jesus is the reflection, emanation, and display of God's glory. He is the "exact imprint" of God's nature. He is the radiance of God's eternal immensity. He is the showcase of the infinite awesomeness of God.

There is a solar flare of Hebrews 1:3 in Revelation 21:23 where it says that the glory of God will illuminate the new heaven and earth, with the Lamb as the lamp. Jesus will be the sun of the world to come! And like the sun, if Jesus is not at the center of our solar system, nothing works. No life results. No balance is found. If the sun is not at the center of our system, everything is chaos, disorder, death.

Also like the sun's superabundant rays, the radiant beams of awesomeness emanating from Jesus are too numerous to count.

But let's try.

Each thing the Bible reveals about Jesus can be considered a single ray of his infinite excellence. We may see the radiance of God's glory in each of his revealed vocations. For instance, is there not expansive brightness in knowing that Christ is our Advocate, the Author and Perfecter of our faith, the Bridegroom, the Deliverer, the Redeemer, the Kinsman Redeemer, the Good Shepherd, the Great High Priest, the Messiah, the Horn of Salvation, the Great Physician, the Son of Man, the Mediator, the second Adam, the resurrected Lord?

Do we not see rays upon rays of light and heat in the facets of his atoning work, knowing he is the Lamb of God, the ransom, the propitiation, the victor, our righteousness?

Are there not sunbeams upon sunbeams within and beside

the symbols of our Savior, when we see he is the Bread of Life, the Chief Cornerstone, the Way and the Truth and the Life, the Gate, the Rock, the Vine?

He was there in the shadows of the days of old, walking through the garden to call Adam to account, wrestling with Jacob, accepting tribute from the prophets and the psalmists who only saw him vaguely, standing in solidarity alongside Shadrach, Meshach, and Abed-nego in the flames of the furnace. Was that Jesus?

> I see him, but not now;
>> I behold him, but not near:
> a star shall come out of Jacob,
>> and a scepter shall rise out of Israel;
> it shall crush the forehead of Moab
>> and break down all the sons of Sheth. (Num. 24:17)

The Son rises, and we see. We see! He is the Bright Morning Star. He is the Light of the World. He is the radiance of the glory of God.

From Jesus the Christ even emanate crosswise excellencies. By this I mean that rays of excellence that might appear contradictory nonetheless converge in Christ who is their unity and reemerge from him in a way that complement each other and compliment him. John Piper, borrowing from Jonathan Edwards, elaborates:

> The glory of Christ, as he appeared among us, consisted not in one attribute or another, and not in one act or another, but in what Jonathan Edwards called "an admirable conjunction of diverse excellencies." In a sermon titled "The Excellency of Christ" Edwards took as his text Revelation 5:5–6 where Christ is compared both to a lion and a lamb. His point was that the unique glory of Christ was that such diverse excellencies (lion and lamb) unite in him. These excellencies are so diverse that they "would have seemed to us utterly incompatible in the same subject." In other words,
>
> • we admire him for his glory, but even more because his glory is mingled with humility;

- we admire him for his transcendence, but even more because his transcendence is accompanied by condescension;
- we admire him for his uncompromising justice, but even more because it is tempered with mercy;
- we admire him for his majesty, but even more because it is a majesty in meekness;
- we admire him because of his equality with God, but even more because as God's equal he nevertheless has a deep reverence for God;
- we admire him because of how worthy he was of all good, but even more because this was accompanied by an amazing patience to suffer evil;
- we admire him because of his sovereign dominion over the world, but even more because this dominion was clothed with a spirit of obedience and submission;
- we love the way he stumped the proud scribes with his wisdom, and we love it even more because he could be simple enough to like children and spend time with them;
- and we admire him because he could still the storm, but even more because he refused to use that power to strike the Samaritans with lightning (Luke 9:54–55) and he refused to use it to get himself down from the cross.

The list could go on and on. But this is enough to illustrate that beauty and excellency in Christ is not a simple thing. It is complex. It is a coming together in one person of the perfect balance and proportion of extremely diverse qualities. And that's what makes Jesus Christ uniquely glorious, excellent, and admirable.[1]

Edwards locates the divergent lines of lion-ness and lamb-ness that cross at Christ. Still there are more.

Jesus is the Priest who is the sacrifice.
Jesus is the Judge who takes the punishment.
Jesus is the Shepherd who is the lamb.
Jesus is the Scapegoat and the paschal lamb.
Jesus is the King who is a servant.
Jesus is the Prince of Peace who comes to bring a sword.

---

[1]John Piper, *God Is the Gospel: Meditations on God's Love as the Gift of Himself* (Wheaton, IL: Crossway, 2005), 52–53.

Jesus is the Alpha and the Omega, the first and last, the beginning
  and the end.
Jesus is the Man who is God.
Jesus is the Prophet who is the Priest who is the King.

The crosswise excellencies of Christ continue unabated. If the
world could not contain all the books that might hold what Jesus
did in his earthly ministry, is it any wonder that we will bask in
his infinite glory for all eternity?

The only way this will not bowl you over is if you think you're
hot stuff. And you are not hot stuff. But Jesus is.

"He upholds the universe by the word of his power," the author of
Hebrews continues (1:3). John 1:1–3 tells us the world was created
by Jesus. We know from the first chapter of Genesis that the world
was created with words. It makes sense he would sustain this creation by lording over it with his word of power still. And there is
a double sense here. Jesus Christ upholds the universe by his powerful word—he says "Stay," and it does—but the ESV's rendering
gives us a clever picture of the universe holding at the "word" of
his power, as if it has heard the mere rumor of Christ's power and
will not dare step out of line.

If Christ controls the universe, by the way, it changes *everything.* Or it should. There is so much now to rethink and reform! If
Christ upholds the universe, we must jettison the dualistic notion
that Satan and God are fighting and the outcome is unsure. I have
read and heard some ideas that leave the impression that these
fighting forces are relying on *our* power to prevail. Can you imagine that? God needing our prayers to uphold his universe? Some
pop-culture attempts at capturing this notion make Jesus seem
like Tinkerbell, down for the count unless the applause of his spec-
tators revives him. Repent of this pathetic fairy Jesus.

If Christ upholds the universe by the word of his power, we
should stop worrying about the end of the world. Is there global
warming? Maybe so, maybe not. But either way, it's not the end of
the world until Jesus says it is. He's got it.

If he upholds the universe by the word of his power, we need
to repent of the arrogance of thinking this world is what we make

of it, of the prideful beliefs that drive "name it and claim it," prosperity gospel, "word of faith," and other man-centered heretical horse puckey.

He upholds the universe by the word of his power!

"After making purification for sins." How excellent is Christ? Well, perfection is required to make purification for sins. But even the most perfect lambs did not eradicate sin for all time. "Every priest stands daily at his service, offering repeatedly the same sacrifices, which can never take away sins" (Heb. 10:11). But "he has no need, like those high priests, to offer sacrifices daily, first for his own sins and then for those of the people, since he did this once for all when he offered up himself" (Heb. 7:27). He must not just be perfect, but *super*perfect.

And he wielded his perfection for us, for our purification.

"He sat down at the right hand of the Majesty on high" (1:3). Why is he seated? Because the work is done. The payment has been made in full; the feat has been accomplished *in toto*.

"Having become as much superior to angels as the name he has inherited is more excellent than theirs" (1:4).

Can I tell you one of the problems with books like *Heaven Is for Real?*[2] Aside from the obvious honesty issues, they very often demote Jesus to a character in heaven like one of the costumed players at Disney World. He is Santa Claus, an attraction of some kind. He is a featured player in heaven in these stories. But in the Scriptures there is no heaven without Jesus. Should we have a heaven without Jesus, it would be no heaven at all. He is all or he is nothing.

Do you recall the cultural fascination with angels? This trend comes and goes in waves, but there was a period in the mid-eighties to early nineties where angel products were all the rage. Angel ornaments, angel figurines, TV shows about angels, books about angels, talk shows talking about angels. Why do people love angels so much? I think it's because they provide a vague sense of spirituality to people that is both pleasant and peaceable, which is

---

[2] Todd Burpo with Lynn Vincent, *Heaven Is for Real: A Little Boy's Astounding Story of His Trip to Heaven and Back* (Nashville: Thomas Nelson, 2010).

to say, not much like the holy encounters we find in the Scriptures. The angels in the Bible say things like "Fear not!" because they apparently do not show up as sweet ladies in pink gowns or rosy-cheeked babies playing harps. It is perhaps going too far to say they are like Peretti's bodybuilder angels, but they invariably provoke a sense of undone-ness. Witness Isaiah 6, for instance.

Also, the angels of pop culture are usually envisioned as catering to us. Certainly, the Scriptures give us an indication that God charges angels with guarding his children, but this is a far cry from the oracular, pandering angels of modern lore. These unbiblical angels more resemble genies.

In almost every instance, the modern fascination with angels is a prideful affront to Jesus's superiority over them. Angels make spirituality about us. But Jesus makes it all about him. He places himself at the center of the universe. He demands a response of love or hatred. You cannot be ambivalent about Jesus, not really (Matt. 12:30).

Jesus surpasses. The buck stops at Jesus. What do you call the fellow who, while sitting down, says things that then happen? The boss.

Jesus says in Matthew 10:33, "Whoever denies me before men, I also will deny before my Father who is in heaven." To love Jesus is to be with him, for him, in him, and by him, and to have life eternal. To reject Jesus is to choose hell.

Why? Because he is superior to angels and all else, and his inherited name is more excellent than the names of angels or any other name.

What name has he inherited? The name above all names!

His is the name *full* of names! He is the Christ, the Lord, the Almighty, the Faithful and True, the Alpha and Omega, Immanuel—God with Us, the Bright Morning Star, the Sun of Righteousness, King of kings and Lord of lords, the Lion of Judah, the Root of David, the Son of David. He is Rabbi, God's Only Begotten Son, the Ancient of Days, the Word of God, the Great I AM.

His name is above all names (Eph. 1:21; Phil. 2:9). His name alone is exalted (Ps. 148:13). There is no other name given under heaven by which we may be saved (Acts 4:12).

If we are to experience the love of God and he to know ours, if we would see genuine revival, if we would begin to seek justice in response to the gracious offering of the Son, we must see the glory of God in the face of Jesus Christ. It is this big, central, radiant Jesus we must believe, worship, and proclaim.

As Calvin says, "Christ is, as it were, a fountain, open to us, from which we may draw what otherwise would lie unprofitably hidden in that deep and secret spring."[3] And, oh, how are hearts are parched! Like the deer pants for the water, our soul longs for Jesus (Ps. 42:1). This is true even in our obliviousness, as we seek satiation in the brackish sludge of anything else. We need the living water, or we will always be thirsty to death. But just as there are infinite sunbeams of glory in Jesus, there are infinite springs of saving goodness in him. So the psalmists sing, "All my springs are in you" (Ps. 87:7).

The deep things of God, personal closeness to God, and secure relationship with God all come from Jesus, the radiance of the glory of God. "All the blessings God has for us are tied up with the work of Christ," D. A. Carson reminds us.[4] Gospel abundance is spilling out of Christ, flowing freely, grace upon grace, one after another. Gospel blessings are both secured in him and gratuitously offered. He lavishes us with the treasure of himself. He bids us come play in the radiance of his wonderfulness. M'Cheyne lures us to swim:

> Unfathomable oceans of grace are in Christ for you. Dive and dive again, you will never come to the bottom of these depths. How many millions of dazzling pearls and gems are at this moment hid in the deep recesses of the ocean caves! But there are unsearchable riches in Christ.[5]

Dane Ortlund shows us how the ocean cavern of Christ's awe-

---

[3] John Calvin, *Institutes of the Christian Religion*, ed. John T. McNeill, trans. Ford Lewis Battles, 2 vols. (Philadelphia: Westminster, 1960), 1:736.

[4] D. A. Carson, *A Call to Spiritual Reformation: Priorities from Paul and His Prayers* (Grand Rapids, MI: Baker, 2006), 189.

[5] Robert Murray M'Cheyne, *Memoir and Remains of Reverend Robert Murray M'Cheyne* (London: W. Middleton, 1845), 240.

someness reaches deeply down before the beginning of time. There is no bottom there, but the farthest we can go is a dizzying depth indeed, and the New Testament books chart the course:

Matthew fulfills the OT's hope for a Messiah, a Christ, an anointed son of David who would save God's people (1:21).

Mark fulfills the OT's hope for a coming Son of God who would inaugurate God's kingdom (1:1, 14–15).

Luke fulfills the OT's longing for God to come and set right the world's injustices—reversing rich and poor, oppressors and oppressed, satisfied and hungry, outsider and insider (19:10).

John fulfills the OT's longing for the tabernacle/temple to do decisively what it was always meant to do—unite God and man in restored fellowship (1:14; 2:21; 14:6).

Acts fulfills the OT by bringing God's mercy to the nations (1:8; 9:15).

Romans fulfills the OT by showing the supreme manifestation of the righteousness of God, in Jesus, bringing resolution to the constant OT tension between God's justice and his mercy (1:17; 3:21–26).

1 Corinthians fulfills the OT by showing, in Christ, the climactic way in which God destroys the wisdom of the wise (1:19).

2 Corinthians fulfills the OT's repeated pattern of strength through weakness (12:9–10), supremely in Christ (13:4), in whom all the promises of God are clinched (1:20).

Galatians fulfills the OT by showing that Jesus' atoning work (3:13) at just the right time (4:4–5) is the reason that the real children of Abraham are those who are of faith (3:7–9).

Ephesians fulfills the OT by revealing the "mystery" long hidden—that Christ, by virtue of his death and resurrection, unites Jews and Gentiles in one renewed people of God (3:5–6).

Philippians fulfills the OT by showing that the church is the real circumcision (3:2–3).

Colossians fulfills the OT by showing that another Adam, likewise made in God's image (1:15), has fulfilled the creation mandate of Genesis 1:28 to bear fruit and increase, so that we who are united to this second Adam can now do what the first Adam failed to do—bearing fruit and multiplying (1:10).

1 and 2 Thessalonians fulfill the OT's hope of judgment on God's enemies by showing that Jesus received this judgment, so

that God's punitive judgment, which is surely coming, now will fall only on those who reject Jesus (1 Thess 5:1–10; 2 Thess 1:5–12).

1 and 2 Timothy fulfill the OT by showing that the true warfare of God's people is not against the Amalekites and Amorites and others but against sin and Satan (1 Tim 1:18; 6:12; 2 Tim 2:3–4), a war that cannot be lost because of the Savior anticipated in the OT (2 Tim 3:15).

Titus fulfills the OT's underachieved efforts to redeem a people for God who are his own possession, zealous for good works (2:11–14).

Philemon fulfills the OT's insistence that love be from the heart (v. 14).

Hebrews fulfills the OT's longing for a perfect priest and final sacrifice to usher in the new covenant (8:1–13).

James fulfills the OT's call for obedience to the law by showing that such obedience is fulfilled in one thing—active love (1:12; 2:8–26).

1 and 2 Peter fulfill the OT's calling to Israel to be a royal priesthood and a holy nation (1 Pet 1:4–12)—a corporate fulfillment that happens only because of another fulfillment that is not only corporate but also individual, this time of Isaiah 52–53 (1 Pet 2:22–25).

1, 2, and 3 John fulfill the OT by showing that through Christ we are once more, like Adam, sons of God, and now able to fulfill the OT law through love (1 John 3:1 and passim).

Jude fulfills the exodus in the OT by showing that ultimately is was Jesus who provided this rescue (Jude 5; cf. 1 Cor 10:4).

Revelation fulfills the OT by showing that Jesus has conquered our great enemy, death, which was introduced in Eden (Rev 1:18; 21:4).[6]

For those who have the neurological condition synesthesia, sensory pathways in the brain may activate each other. For instance, someone with synesthesia may always see the number four as blue, or they may always smell apples when they hear a certain piece of music. One cognitive thread activates another. One sense stirs another.

---

[6] Dane Ortlund, "The New Testament's Multi-Dimensional Fulfillment of the Old," in *Strawberry-Rhubarb Theology* (blog), October 26, 2011, http://dogmadoxa.blogspot.com/2011/10/new-testaments-multi-dimensional.html.

There is a Spiritual sense in which beholding Jesus is like this. Because he plays in ten thousand places, he also plays in ten thousand ways in one place. To read his words is to see his face smiling and his hand extended. To see his face is to hear the angels crying "Holy!" To receive him one way is to receive him in so many others. He comes as Lord over us and Savior to us. He is a lion for us and a lamb to us. He is a lamb for us and a lion to us. He touches us, and we smell the sweet fragrance of his glory. On the day—may it come this very next second!—that we see him face to face, we will know as we are known, and in the white hot heat of his divine radiance, as the weight of God's fullness envelops us in the infinite lift of rapturous bliss, his excellencies will stir all our affections, senses, neural pathways, receivers, spiritual antennae, and instincts, drawing to the surface of our glorified selves a synesthesia so ecstatically overwhelming, we will erupt in endless exultation forever after.

The gospel is the news that God saves sinners through the life, death, and resurrection of Jesus Christ. Therein are depths within depths. Therein are multitudes. Therein are crosswise excellencies upon crosswise excellencies, highlighting each other, playing off each other, refracting and reflecting, compassing the universe in crosshatched beauty, a dance of radiance that will never rest, for the earth will be covered with his glory undeniable. From him and to him and through him and for him are all things. He is before all things, and in him all things hold together (Col. 1:17), that God may be all in all (1 Cor. 15:28).

Our brother Calvin may have the next-to-last word:

> We see that our whole salvation and all its parts are comprehended in Christ. We should therefore take care not to derive the least portion of it from anywhere else. If we seek salvation, we are taught by the very name of Jesus that it is of him. If we seek any other gifts of the Spirit, they will be found in his anointing. If we seek strength, it lies in his dominion; if purity, in his conception; if gentleness, it appears in his birth. For by his birth he was made like us in all respects, that he might learn to feel our pain. If we seek redemption, it lies in his passion; if acquittal, in

his condemnation; if remission of the curse, in his cross; if satisfaction, in his sacrifice; if purification, in his blood; if reconciliation, in his descent into hell; if mortification of the flesh, in his tomb; if newness of life, in his resurrection; if immortality, in the same; if inheritance of the Heavenly Kingdom, in his entrance into heaven; if protection, if security, if abundant supply of all blessings, in his Kingdom; if untroubled expectation of judgment, in the power given to him to judge. In short, since rich store of every kind of good abounds in him, let us drink our fill from this fountain, and from no other.[7]

And the last word ever after shall be: Soli Deo Gloria.

---

[7]Calvin, *Institutes*, 1:527.

Conclusion

"To grow in your passion for what Jesus has done, increase your understanding of what He has done. Never be content with your grasp of the gospel. The gospel is life-permeating, world-altering, universe-changing truth. It has more facets than any diamond. Its depths man will never exhaust."—C. J. Mahaney[1]

Are we in danger of gospel fatigue? This is a real danger. Not that the gospel may be worn out, but that we may grow tired of hearing about it. Some believe the gospel is not for every square inch of existence but for special occasions. Some believe we may reduce or hinder its power from overuse. Some speak as if we must cordon it off from ordinary means lest we dull or tarnish it. These all think too little of the gospel.

But doesn't the author of Hebrews tell us to move on?

> Anyone who lives on milk, being still an infant, is not acquainted with the teaching about righteousness. But solid food is for the mature, who by constant use have trained themselves to distinguish good from evil. (Heb. 5:13–14 NIV)

> Therefore let us leave the elementary teachings about Christ and go on to maturity, not laying again the foundation of repentance from acts that lead to death, and of faith in God, instruction about baptisms, the laying on of hands, the resurrection of the dead, and eternal judgment. (Heb. 6:1–2 NIV)

The problem is that these passages don't mean what many think they do. Those who want to handle the gospel with kid gloves posit them as proof of the idea that Christians ought to "graduate from the gospel." Not only do we not find this idea anywhere else in Scripture, it is not the point of these passages from Hebrews either, despite appearing so to the casual reader. Some context is helpful.

---

[1]C. J. Mahaney, *The Cross Centered Life: Keeping the Gospel the Main Thing* (Colorado Springs: Multnomah, 2002), 67.

In Hebrews 5:12, the author writes, "Though by this time you ought to be teachers, you have need again for someone to teach you the elementary principles of the oracles of God" (NASB) The dilemma is seeing how the recipients of the letter would need to both relearn the elementary principles of the oracles of God and leave the elementary teachings about Christ. Unless the author is speaking out of both sides of his mouth, these must mean two different things.

What does the "foundation" we're told not to lay again consist of? "Repentance from acts that lead to death, and of faith in God, instruction about baptisms, the laying on of hands, the resurrection of the dead, and eternal judgment." John Piper writes this:

> So evidently there is a difference between the teaching that they need in 5:12 and the laying again of a foundation in 6:1. One they need and one they don't. What's the difference?
>
> I think the teaching they need about the basics (5:12) is how to use these basics for Christ's sake to press on to maturity. But laying a foundation again, I think, implies that they are losing sight of the basics about Christ and are beginning to occupy themselves with Old Testament and Jewish truths that were used as the foundation for presenting and understanding Christ. And the writer doesn't want them to go that far back.
>
> Let me explain. In this writer's mind, laying a foundation for the understanding of Christ is different from teaching about how to live in Christ on the basis of that foundation. The foundation he has in mind is described in 6:1d–2. The striking thing about this list is that it is not distinctively Christian. It is made up of foundational Old Testament and Jewish truths and practices that the readers probably built on when they were converted.[2]

John Calvin concurs, writing of this passage:

> He bids them to leave these rudiments, not that the faithful are ever to forget them, but that they are not to remain in them; and this idea appears more clear from what follows, the comparison of a foundation; for in building a house we must never leave the

---

[2]John Piper, "Let Us Press on to Maturity," *Desiring God Online*, October 6, 1996), http://www.desiringgod.org/resource-library/sermons/let-us-press-on-to-maturity.

foundation; and yet to be always engaged in laying it, would be ridiculous. For as the foundation is laid for the sake of what is built on it, he who is occupied in laying it and proceeds not to the superstruction, wearies himself with foolish and useless labor.[3]

I would sum it up this way: You never leave the foundation, but you only lay the foundation once. Or perhaps this way: At the cross, you are saved once for all time. Don't get resaved. Walk in your salvation.

Tullian Tchividjian puts it this way:

> Sanctification is a grueling process. But it's NOT the process of moving beyond the reality of our justification but rather moving deeper into the reality of our justification. If sanctification could be likened to our responsibility to swim, justification is the pool we swim in. Sanctification is the hard work of going back to the certainty of our already secured pardon in Christ and hitting the refresh button over and over.[4]

In any event, I believe the passages from Hebrews cited don't mean the gospel is the ABCs of the Christian life and now we need to buckle down and learn the hard stuff. Instead, they are calls to grow in the gospel, not away from it.

What happens to us when we drink deeply from the gospel, when we stare at its glory like angels do? According to 2 Corinthians 3:18, we ourselves transform from one degree of glory to another when we behold Jesus.

I like Romans 12:11's command in the RSV to "be aglow with the Spirit." That may or may not be the most accurate translation. The ESV prefers "be fervent in spirit," which is different but not incompatible with the RSV. "Be aglow with the Spirit" is certainly a biblical thought. "Those who look to him are radiant," in Psalm 34:5, comes to mind. His radiance can be reflected. We can be aglow with him, if we would but look and really see.

The danger lies in seeing in and through the crucifixion and

---

[3]John Calvin, *Commentaries on the Epistle of Paul the Apostle to the Hebrews*, trans. and ed. John Owen, Christian Classics Ethereal Library, http://www.ccel.org/ccel/calvin/calcom44.i.html.
[4]Tullian Tchividjian, "Work Hard! But in Which Direction?" *Liberate* (blog), June 8, 2011, http://thegospelcoalition.org/blogs/tullian/2011/06/08/work-hard-but-in-which-direction/.

resurrection and ending up not seeing the crucifixion and resurrection. Let us remember that the deep gospel delivered to us was proclaimed not with eloquent speech and not by sophisticated men. They simply wielded fire. Fire is a simple thing that complicates matters quickly. And so is the good news.

So let us feel the deep, deep wonder of the very simple precept, "If you confess with your mouth that Jesus is Lord and believe in your heart that God raised him from the dead, you will be saved" (Rom. 10:9). It is a simple enough announcement that the entire riches of Christ may be received with a mustard seed–sized faith. But the mustard seed gives way to bird-abundant habitat (Matt. 13:32). The gospel is the "little bit" that fills and takes over the world (Matt. 13:33; Col. 1:5–6).

Leon Morris writes:

> The chief impression that a study of the atonement leaves with us is that of the many-sidedness of Christ's work for men. When he died for us on the cross, he did something so infinitely wonderful that it is impossible to comprehend it in its fulness. However man's need be understood, that need is fully and abundantly met in Christ. The New Testament writers are like men who ransack their vocabulary to find words which will bring out some small fraction of the mighty thing that God has done for us. And yet, though it is so complex and so difficult, it may be put very simply: "the life which I now live in the flesh I live by the faith of the Son of God, who loved me and gave himself for me" (Gal. 2:20).[5]

Though the gospel is simple, we can't wear it out, because we can't wear out Jesus.

All of him for all of us. It is true. It is ours to repent and believe.

---

[5] Leon Morris, *The Cross in the New Testament* (Grand Rapids, MI: Eerdmans, 1965), 419.

Scripture Index

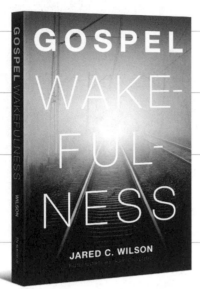

Do you ever feel like your desire for God is waning?

Are you numb to the routine of church?

What does it mean to be truly awakened to the wonder of the gospel?

Jared Wilson contends that we must be regularly engaged and engaging others with the good news of the sacrificing, dying, rising, exalted person of Jesus Christ. Wilson reminds us of the death-proof, fail-proof King of kings who is before all things and in all things and holding all things together, and of the Spirit's power to quicken our hearts and captivate our imaginations. The message of *Gospel Wakefulness* will make numbness the exception and reawaken us to the multifaceted brilliance of the gospel.

"My eyes filled with tears and my heart flooded with joy on numerous occasions. It's been a long time since a book created the emotion in me that this book has."
> **MATT CHANDLER,** Lead Pastor, The Village Church, Dallas, Texas; author, *The Explicit Gospel*

"Writing with passion and clarity, Wilson shines the light of Christ on every page."
> **ED STETZER,** President, LifeWay Research

"Wilson's book changes how we see the gospel and reminds us of just how amazing grace is."
> **GREG SURRATT,** Senior Pastor, Seacoast Church, Mt. Pleasant, South Carolina